Susan's Cheesecakes

A collection of homemade recipes from Susan Eckles

With photographs by Jill Mansfield

Dedication

To My Children:

Renee Keller Cavanaugh

William Joseph Keller

Gail Keller Henderson

Melody Keller Depasquale

Nicholas Robert Walluck

My kitchen is my sanctuary…always has been. It's where I go to collect my thoughts, find peace, and feel nurtured. Some people find inspiration in their garden and others in their workshop - I find it in my kitchen. It's where I go to feel happy, excited and creative.

I've always loved baking, and cheesecake is my choice dessert. Whether it's the holidays, a birthday or other special occasion, I always look forward to sharing something I love with people I love.

Like most small businesses, I started operating out of my home. I began taking orders from friends and family and word spread about my cheesecakes. Then when my sons got into the restaurant business, I decided to supply them with my cheesecakes.

I have, over the years, entertained the notion of publishing a cookbook about cheesecakes. After all, I've been developing recipes, collecting pictures and dreaming about the possibility of sharing my ideas with others. It seemed difficult, daunting in fact. Where do I start, how do I do this...it never seemed like the right time.

Then one evening, my husband and I were watching a documentary entitled *Becoming Warren Buffett.* Seeing his story and hearing his words, "take what you enjoy doing and go for it," was the catalyst for creating this cookbook. Thank you Warren Buffett for your inspiration.

I reside in Tullahoma, Tennessee with my husband George, and at 69 I am living my life to the fullest. It is never too late to live the life you want, to help people less fortunate than yourself, and to change the world with one little kindness at a time. I believe God gives us all something special, and he wants us to share it with others. I hope you enjoy sharing these recipes with the ones you love.

A portion of the proceeds of this book will go to help the beautiful children at St. Jude's Children's Hospital in Memphis, Tennessee.

Table of Contents

Cheesecake How To's & Other Helpful Hints - 5
    Making the Crust 8
    Crust Options 8
    Making the Batter 9
    Removing From The Pan 10
    How to Prevent Cracking 11
    Making Chantilly Cream 12

The Great Depression Cheesecake - 15
    The Great Depression 19

All Time Favorites - 21
    Raspberry White Chocolate 23
    Zesty Lemon Cream 25
    Toasted Almond 27
    Coconut Cream 29
    Key Lime 31
    Butter Pecan 33
    Pineapple 35
    Peaches & Cream 37

Chocolate, Chocolate & More Chocolate - 39
    Triple Chocolate Chip 41
    Espresso with a Chocolate Swirl 43
    Chocolate Malted 47
    Chocolate Chip Cookie 49
    Recipe For Chocolate Chip Cookies . . . 51
    German Chocolate 53
    Peanut Butter Cup 55

Special Occasion & Seasonal - 57

    Banana Rum 59

    Black Forest 61

    Blue Pear 63

    Dazzle Berry 65

    Pumpkin Spice 67

    Dead Velvet 69

    Crème Brule 73

    Eggnog 77

    Wedding Cake 79

    Groom's Cake 81

Kids At Heart - 83

    Neapolitan 85

    Orange Crème Pop 87

    Peanut Butter & Jelly 89

    S'more 91

    Caramel Apple 93

    Recipe For Burnt Caramel Sauce 95

Cheesecake How To's & Other Helpful Hints

Here are a few tips that I have found to be most helpful:

- Please read the entire recipe before you start. Nothing is more frustrating than being halfway through the cake-making process and realizing you don't have a key ingredient – *ugh!*

- Check your oven to make sure 350 degrees is in fact 350 degrees.

- Always preheat your oven!

- I recommend all ingredients be at room temperature before starting.

- I use salted butter in my recipes. I like the results.

- I also use only real vanilla extract.

- I don't recommend using low-fat; fat-free; or any other dairy substitute products for the "real thing." Quality ingredients will yield a quality product.

- To ensure a smooth batter, I process the ingredients using a food processor with at least a 10 cup capacity.

- Be sure to place the bottom of the spring-form pan in correctly (the bottom of the pan is inverted so that the cheesecake is easy to remove).

- All of the recipes in this book use a 10 inch spring-form pan.

- I also place my cheesecake on top of a solid 12 inch pizza pan. This will catch any excess butter that might drip.

- I always put a shallow pan of water (about 4 cups) on the bottom shelf of the oven - this helps prevent cracking.

- I find using an offset baking/icing spatula with a metal blade to be extremely helpful when removing the cake from the spring-form pan.

- Please note that cheesecakes need to be refrigerated several hours or overnight before serving.

- To slice your cheesecake cleanly, use a large, sharp, hot knife. Slice downward through the crust, then pull knife toward you - this will prevent clumping. Wipe your knife clean with a hot towel after each slice.

- *Relax and have fun!* Create your own favorite flavor combinations.

Making the Crust

Put all dry ingredients in a mixing bowl and stir to incorporate. Add in the melted butter and stir until all ingredients are combined. The crumbs will be moist.

Pour the crust mixture into the middle of a 10-inch spring-form type pan. Use your fingers to spread the crumbs evenly in the bottom of the pan. Then, using the palm of your hand, press the crumbs firmly going all the way to the edge of the pan.

Place the prepared crust on top of another pan to prevent leakage into your oven.

Crust Options

There are many options for crust ingredients. The most popular is the regular graham cracker crumb crust. However, I also love using chocolate graham cracker crumbs, gingersnap cookie crumbs, vanilla wafer cookie crumbs and shortbread cookie crumbs. Almost any cookie crumbs can be used. I use my food processor to turn cookies into crumbs - just be sure that you have 2 cups of crumbs when making your cheesecake crust.

Making the Batter

Place all ingredients except for the eggs in the work bowl of the processor. *Note: all ingredients should be at room temperature.* Mix on high until the batter is smooth.

Add the eggs, one at a time and mix on high speed until you have a smooth, lump-free batter.

Please know that to achieve best results, you will need to stop processing, remove the top of the work bowl, and using a plastic spatula – scrape down the sides of the work bowl and check for lumps throughout the mixing process.

Pour the mixture into the spring-form pan on top of the unbaked crust.

Bake on the middle rack in the oven for approximately one hour or until it is slightly brown around the edges. Remove the pan from the oven and then let it sit for at least one or two hours until it is at room temperature, then refrigerate. I leave it in the refrigerator for several hours or overnight. This creates a firm cheesecake that will allow placement of the topping later.

Removing From The Pan

When the cake is completely cold, use an offset baking/icing spatula with a metal blade (or knife) and run it around the inside edges of the pan to loosen the cake from the sides of the pan.

Once you feel that the cake has been loosened from the sides of the spring-form pan, open the spring to release the cake. Gently lift the sides of the pan off of the cake.

Using the same spatula or knife, insert it between the crust and the bottom of the pan. Gently glide the metal spatula or knife under the crust and around to loosen it from the bottom of the pan. Carefully slide the cake onto your serving plate.

How to Prevent Cracking

Most of the cheesecakes I bake end up being topped with something luscious like Chantilly Cream or Rich Chocolate Ganache. So, if a cake cracks, it doesn't really bother me; it will be hidden under the topping and no one will be the wiser.

However, cheesecakes tend to crack as they cool, and despite your best efforts, you might end up with a crack on top - not the most ideal for presentations, but it certainly won't affect the flavor.

If you are baking a cheesecake that is not covered with a topping and you want to minimize the risk for cracking, here are a few suggestions:

- Put a pan of water on the bottom shelf of the oven while you are baking. This will create steam, keeping your cake moist and preventing cracking. I always do this step for all my cheesecakes.

- As soon as you remove your cake from the oven, let it sit for 5 to 10 minutes. Then insert a sharp knife between the side of the pan and your cake, slide the knife around the sides to loosen the cake from the side of the pan. Do this while the cake is still hot. Cross your fingers! Sometimes it works very well.

Making Chantilly Cream

 Using a 1 quart mixing bowl and hand mixer, combine the softened cream cheese, powdered sugar and vanilla extract.

 Whip on high until smooth.

 Add heavy whipping cream to cream cheese mixture and whip on high until stiff peaks form.

 Be sure that your cheesecake is completely cooled (or preferably cold) before topping with Chantilly Cream. For best results, keep topped cheesecake refrigerated until time to serve.

The Great Depression Cheesecake

During my childhood, as far back as I can remember, I can hear my grandmother's voice saying,
> *"You're lucky to have food on ye plate young lady, be thankful that you didn't have to live through the 'Great Depression' when all you had to eat was cornbread and buttermilk to save ye life. If you get hungry enough, ye will eat what's on your plate and be proud ye got it."*

As a child I would listen and pay attention to my elders tell stories about how bad the times were in the South – when cornbread and buttermilk saved many a life.
> *"Yes sir little lady, cornbread and buttermilk kept many a man from starvation. Young'uns today need to thank their lucky stars that they were spared the crash of 1929."*

Well, I guess I should thank my lucky stars, but truth be known, my siblings and I were as poor as church mice and most of the time hungry enough to eat dirt. To hear them tell it though, we had it better and perhaps we did.

They would preach about the Great Depression as if it were a war that they had fought long ago and had survived and for which they had received the Purple Heart. The tempo of their voices would rise and fall as each one spoke of a specific "battle." Their body language would convey the swell of pride of overcoming a particular obstacle then deflate just as quickly when reliving their shortcomings.
> *"Remember when we barely made it by the skin of our teeth? Remember when we got so hungry we waited till old man Warren's cows 'udders were full as a tick? We'd sneaked in his barn and milk that cow straight into our glasses drinking it warm and fresher than the morning dew. Milk running down our chins trying to get away from old man Warren; we were young and old man Warren was not. We got our lickin' for stealing, but it was worth it. Our stomachs weren't growling anymore."*

In those days the man of the house was revered and obeyed like a religion. And like religion, it was practiced daily. The menfolk would be served first at the dinner table. They would eat and talk about their failing crops, and after a while the fruit jar would make its appearance with its clear intoxicating liquid – moonshine. After a bit, the conversation would shift back in time to the Great Depression with its laughter and tears - all the while the men were taking turns with the white lightning.

The women of the South have often been referred to as Steel Magnolias, tough as nails and soft as a boll of cotton. They didn't need, nor did they have the time, to pass around the fruit jar. Their drink of choice was the house wine of the South "sweet tea." They were too busy picking blackberries to make jam, teaching their daughters how to bake cornbread, churning buttermilk for the family, or making fresh peach cobbler for the church potluck. Daughters were taught that "keeping up ye figure, and looking pretty" were vitally important priorities. I remember many times watching my great aunts and my grandmother reach under the fireplace or the old potbelly stove to retrieve black soot and dab on the gray hair that was interfering with their youth.

My grandmother would often give me advice.
> *"Susan, remember the way to a man's heart is through his stomach, listen to ye momma now. This way ye can find yerself a good, Christian man that will bring home a paycheck."*

Over the years I have told these stories, as they had been told to me. I have tried to share the history of the South during the depression of 1929 and the strong will of the people to survive. The idea of taking the lifesaving "cornbread and buttermilk" and reinventing it into an elegant dessert was my daughter Renée's idea.

Even though my grandmother had often said, *"You can't make a silk purse out of a sow's ear,"* I decided to try anyway. I took cornbread and buttermilk and transformed it into a cheesecake. The crust is a crunchy sweet cornmeal and the cheesecake is a rich buttermilk batter. The blackberries have been soaked with moonshine and folded into a sweet jam. We decided to call it the Great Depression Cheesecake. It carries with it the nostalgic dreams of the past and the hope for a better tomorrow.

The Great Depression

Served With Blackberry Moonshine Sauce

Crust

1 cup all purpose flour
1 cup yellow corn meal
1½ sticks butter, melted
1 teaspoon salt
¾ cup sugar

- Preheat oven to 400 degrees
- Combine all dry ingredients in a bowl
- Add the melted butter
- Mix together until ingredients are combined. This will be a moist mixture
- Using your hands, press mixture evenly into the bottom of a 10 inch spring form pan
- Place spring form pan on top of a cookie sheet or pizza pan – this will prevent butter from dripping onto your oven
- Bake for 15-20 minutes. It will be golden brown around the edges will be very soft to the touch
- Set aside to cool for at least 20 minutes. Crust will become more firm as it cools

Batter

1 – 14 ounce can sweetened condensed milk
2 cups sour cream
3 – 8 ounce packages cream cheese
1 tablespoon vanilla extract
2 tablespoons corn starch
6 large eggs
2 cups whole buttermilk

- Preheat oven to 350 degrees
- Using at least a 10 cup capacity food processor, place all ingredients EXCEPT eggs and buttermilk into the work bowl
- Process on high for about 1 to 2 minutes or until batter is smooth and lump free
- While still processing mixture, start adding the eggs – one at a time
- Please know that to achieve best results, you will need to stop processing, remove top of machine, and using a spatula – scrape down the sides of the work bowl and check for lumps throughout the mixing process.
- Continue to process mixture until it is smooth and free of lumps – about 2 minutes.
- Once batter is smooth, reduce the speed to medium/medium low and add the buttermilk slowly (continue to process)
- Process for 15 seconds just until the buttermilk is completely incorporated
- This will be a very thin mixture
- Pour batter on top of your crust that has cooled – keep spring form pan on top of cookie sheet or pizza pan
- Bake for at least 1 hour. Edges of cake will rise slightly and turn a golden brown
- After baking, remove pan from oven and let sit until it is room temperature (about 1½ to 2 hours)
- Then place cheesecake in the refrigerator (while still in spring form pan) for several hours or overnight

Topping

1 cup blackberry jam or preserves
2 tablespoons of moonshine or blackberry liquor (optional)

- Heat ingredients in a small saucepan over medium to medium high heat stirring constantly
- Sauce should be smooth and rapidly boiling for 30 seconds
- Remove from heat and set aside

To Serve

- Remove cheesecake from spring form pan and transfer to platter
- *Option 1:* Pour sauce on top of the cake, spread evenly, top with fresh, plump blackberries
- *Option 2:* Slice cake and plate each piece, drizzle sauce on top of each piece and top with berries

All Time Favorites

The Raspberry White Chocolate Cheesecake was the first flavor that I experimented with after perfecting the traditional, basic cheesecake. This was more than 20 years ago. I wanted to try to create something different, something beautiful, something delicious. This is probably the most popular cheesecake that I do. Besides being a year-round favorite, it is also very pretty.

Raspberry White Chocolate
Served With Raspberry Sauce

Crust

2 cups graham cracker crumbs
½ cup sugar
1 stick butter, melted

- Combine all dry ingredients in a bowl
- Pour melted butter over dry ingredients
- Mix together until all ingredients are combined
- Using your hands, press mixture evenly into the bottom of a 10 inch spring form pan
- Place spring form pan on top of a cookie sheet or pizza pan - this will prevent butter from dripping onto your oven
- Set aside

Batter

3 – 8 ounces packages cream cheese
2 cups sour cream
1 – 14 ounce can sweetened condensed milk
1 tablespoon vanilla extract
4 large eggs
1 cup white chocolate chips

- Preheat oven to 350 degrees
- Using at least a 10 cup capacity food processor, place all ingredients EXCEPT eggs and white chocolate chips into the work bowl
- Process on high for about 1-2 minutes or until batter is smooth and lump free
- While still processing mixture, start adding the eggs - one at a time
- Please know that to achieve best results, you will need to stop processing, remove top of machine, and using a spatula, scrape down the sides of the work bowl and check for lumps
- Continue to process mixture until it is smooth and free of lumps
- Add white chocolate chips and pulse several times to evenly distribute
- Pour batter on top of crust
- Bake for at least 1 hour or until you notice that the edges of the cake have risen slightly and are golden brown
- Remove pan from oven and let sit until it is room temperature (about 1½ - 2 hours)
- Place in refrigerator while still in spring form pan for several hours or overnight

Topping

1 cup raspberry jam or preserves
2 tablespoons raspberry liquor (Chambord) - *optional*
Fresh raspberries

- Heat the jam or preserves in a small sauce pan over medium heat until sauce reaches a boil and it is smooth
- Remove from heat and add raspberry liquor (if desired) – stir to combine
- Pour warm sauce over cold cheesecake while cheesecake is still in the pan
- Raspberries are very fragile, rinse them gently and let them dry on their own on a paper towel - for best results arrange berries on cake while sauce is still warm

To Serve

- Carefully remove cheesecake from spring form pan and transfer to platter prior to serving

This Lemon Cream Cheesecake is great any time of the year. A sunny yellow slice is the perfect ending to any meal. The addition of gelatin in half the batter is delightful because you get two different textures and an intense lemon flavor.

Zesty Lemon Cream

Served With Chantilly Cream

Crust

2 cups graham cracker crumbs
½ cup sugar
1 stick butter, melted

- Combine all dry ingredients in a bowl
- Pour melted butter over dry ingredients
- Mix together until all ingredients are combined
- Using your hands, press mixture evenly into the bottom of a 10 inch spring form pan
- Place spring form pan on top of a cookie sheet or pizza pan - this will prevent butter from dripping onto your oven
- Set aside

Batter

1 small package (3 ounces) lemon gelatin
½ cup water
3 – 8 ounces packages cream cheese
2 cups sour cream
1 – 14 ounce can sweetened condensed milk
1 tablespoon vanilla extract
1 teaspoon lemon extract
4 large eggs

- Place ½ cup of water into a small sauce pan and bring to a boil
- Add the gelatin to the boiling water, remove pan from heat, stir constantly until gelatin is completely dissolved – set aside *(Note: gelatin mixture needs to stay liquid, if it sits too long it may congeal in which case you will need to reheat slightly to return it to a liquid form)*
- Using at least a 10 cup capacity food processor, place all remaining ingredients EXCEPT eggs, (and gelatin mixture) into the work bowl
- Process on high for about 1-2 minutes or until batter is smooth and lump free
- While still processing mixture, start adding the eggs - one at a time
- Please know that to achieve best results, you will need to stop processing, remove top of machine, and using a spatula, scrape down the sides of the work bowl and check for lumps
- Continue to process mixture until it is smooth and free of lumps
- Pour half of the batter on top of the crust
- Return container to processor, add the gelatin mixture to the remaining batter and process just until combined – do not over mix – this batter will be a light yellow color
- Pour this batter on top of the first layer (in a circular motion) to create a swirl pattern
- Bake for at least 1 hour or until you notice that the edges of the cake have risen slightly and are golden brown
- Remove pan from oven and let sit until it is room temperature (about 1½ - 2 hours)
- Place in refrigerator while still in spring form pan for several hours or overnight

Topping

4 ounces cream cheese
⅓ cup powdered sugar
1 teaspoon vanilla extract
½ teaspoon lemon extract
2 – 4 drops yellow food coloring
1 cup heavy whipping cream

- Put cream cheese, powdered sugar, vanilla and lemon extracts and the food coloring in a 1 quart mixing bowl *(Note: using the food coloring is optional; however, it will create a beautiful yellow color that will enhance the presentation)*
- Using a hand mixer, whip on high until smooth
- Add heavy whipping cream and whip on high until stiff peaks form

To Serve

The zest of 1 – 2 lemons

- Remove cheesecake from spring form pan and transfer to platter
- Swirl Chantilly Cream evenly on top of cake
- Zest the lemons directly on top of the Chantilly Cream avoiding the bitter white pith

You will find layer of almond flavor throughout this recipe. The crust is especially crunchy with the additional of almonds. The cheesecake itself is smooth and lightly flavored with almond and vanilla. The Chantilly cream topping is enhanced by toasted almond slivers. This recipe can be adapted by removing the almond extract and replacing it with 1/3 cup unsweetened cocoa powder and 2 tablespoons instant coffee. This Chocolate Mocha Almond version is delicious too.

Toasted Almond
Served With Chantilly Cream

Crust

2 cups graham cracker crumbs

½ cup sugar

½ cup finely chopped toasted almonds

1 stick butter, melted

- Combine all dry ingredients in a bowl
- Pour melted butter over dry ingredients
- Mix together until all ingredients are combined
- Using your hands, press mixture evenly into the bottom of a 10 inch spring form pan
- Place spring form pan on top of a cookie sheet or pizza pan - this will prevent butter from dripping onto your oven
- Set aside

Batter

3 – 8 ounces packages cream cheese

2 cups sour cream

1 – 14 ounce can sweetened condensed milk

1 tablespoon vanilla extract

1 teaspoon almond extract

4 large eggs

- Preheat oven to 350 degrees
- Using at least a 10 cup capacity food processor, place all ingredients EXCEPT eggs into the work bowl
- Process on high for about 1-2 minutes or until batter is smooth and lump free
- While still processing mixture, start adding the eggs - one at a time
- Please know that to achieve best results, you will need to stop processing, remove top of machine, and using a spatula, scrape down the sides of the work bowl and check for lumps
- Continue to process mixture until it is smooth and free of lumps
- Pour batter on top of crust
- Bake for at least 1 hour or until you notice that the edges of the cake have risen slightly and are golden brown
- Remove pan from oven and let sit until it is room temperature (about 1½ - 2 hours)
- Place in refrigerator while still in spring form pan for several hours or overnight

Topping

4 ounces cream cheese

⅓ cup powdered sugar

1 teaspoon vanilla extract

1 cup heavy whipping cream

- Put cream cheese, powdered sugar and vanilla extract in a 1 quart mixing bowl
- Using a hand mixer, whip on high until smooth
- Add heavy whipping cream and whip on high until stiff peaks form

To Serve

½ cup toasted slivered almonds

- Remove cheesecake from spring form pan and transfer to platter
- Spread Chantilly Cream evenly on top of cake
- Sprinkle the top with the toasted slivered almonds

The Coconut Cream Cheesecake is a coconut lovers dream! The tropical flavor of coconut is highlighted throughout. From the chewy texture of the crust to the lightly toasted topping, this cake takes center stage on warm, summer nights.

Coconut Cream — Served With Chantilly Cream

Crust

2 cups graham cracker crumbs
½ cup sugar
½ cup finely chopped dried coconut
1 stick butter, melted

- Combine all dry ingredients in a bowl
- Pour melted butter over dry ingredients
- Mix together until all ingredients are combined
- Using your hands, press mixture evenly into the bottom of a 10 inch spring form pan
- Place spring form pan on top of a cookie sheet or pizza pan - this will prevent butter from dripping onto your oven
- Set aside

Batter

3 – 8 ounces packages cream cheese
2 cups sour cream
1 – 14 ounce can sweetened condensed milk
1 tablespoon vanilla extract
1 teaspoon coconut extract
½ cup finely chopped dried coconut
4 large eggs

- Preheat oven to 350 degrees
- Using at least a 10 cup capacity food processor, place all ingredients EXCEPT dried coconut and eggs into the work bowl
- Process on high for about 1-2 minutes or until batter is smooth and lump free
- While still processing mixture, start adding the eggs - one at a time
- Please know that to achieve best results, you will need to stop processing, remove top of machine, and using a spatula, scrape down the sides of the work bowl and check for lumps
- Continue to process mixture until it is smooth and free of lumps
- Once you are lump free, add the dried coconut and process just until combined – do not over process
- Pour batter on top of crust
- Bake for about 1 hour or until you notice that the edges of the cake have risen slightly and are golden brown
- Remove pan from oven and let sit until it is room temperature (about 1½ - 2 hours)
- Then place in refrigerator while still in spring form pan for several hours or overnight

Topping

4 ounces cream cheese
⅓ cup powdered sugar
1 teaspoon vanilla extract
1 cup heavy whipping cream

- Put cream cheese, powdered sugar and vanilla extract in a 1 quart mixing bowl
- Using a hand mixer, whip on high until smooth
- Add heavy whipping cream and whip on high until stiff peaks form

To Serve

½ cup toasted dried coconut

- Remove cheesecake from spring form pan and transfer to platter
- Spread Chantilly Cream evenly on top of cake
- Sprinkle the top with the toasted coconut

Key Lime Pie is one of the most refreshing desserts. It's tangy, citrus taste is a nice compliment to the heat of summer. This is a traditional cheesecake with a tempting key lime topping. You will need to allow extra time for the topping to cool, but it sets up nicely.

Key Lime

Served With Key Lime Topping

Crust

2 cups graham cracker crumbs

½ cup sugar

1 stick butter, melted

- Combine all dry ingredients in a bowl
- Pour melted butter over dry ingredients
- Mix together until all ingredients are combined
- Using your hands, press mixture evenly into the bottom of a 10 inch spring form pan
- Place spring form pan on top of a cookie sheet or pizza pan - this will prevent butter from dripping onto your oven
- Set aside

Batter

3 – 8 ounces packages cream cheese

2 cups sour cream

1 – 14 ounce can sweetened condensed milk

1 tablespoon vanilla extract

4 large eggs

- Preheat oven to 350 degrees
- Using at least a 10 cup capacity food processor, place all ingredients EXCEPT eggs into the work bowl
- Process on high for about 1-2 minutes or until batter is smooth and lump free
- While still processing mixture, start adding the eggs - one at a time
- Please know that to achieve best results, you will need to stop processing, remove top of machine, and using a spatula, scrape down the sides of the work bowl and check for lumps
- Continue to process mixture until it is smooth and free of lumps
- Pour batter on top of crust
- Bake for about 1 hour or until you notice that the edges of the cake have risen slightly and are golden brown NOTE: *Just before your cheesecake is ready to come out of the oven, prepare the key lime topping as directed below. Do not allow cake to cool – immediately pour the Key Lime mixture on top of your hot cheesecake*

Topping

1-14 ounce can sweetened condensed milk

3 egg yolks

½ cup freshly squeezed key lime juice

1 drop green food coloring

- In a 1 quart mixing bowl add the sweetened condensed milk, egg yolks and 1 drop of green food coloring.
- Using a whisk, mix together until the egg yolks are well incorporated – the mixture will be a slight green color
- Whisk in the key lime juice – you will notice that the mixture will become thicker
- Pour mixture on top of your hot cheesecake and spread evenly
- Note: to help prevent cracking, gently slide a knife between the cake and the side of the pan and go around the edge to release the cake from the sides of the pan
- Allow finished cheesecake to sit at room temperature (1½ - 2 hours) then refrigerate several hours or overnight

To Serve

Whipped cream, fresh berries, kiwi, or thinly sliced limes – *use your imagination*

- Remove cheesecake from spring form pan and transfer to platter
- Serve as it or add any of the suggested toppings for added interest and presentation

This cheesecake is like eating a bowl of butter pecan ice cream. It is so smooth and buttery – I love it! With its maple flavored Chantilly cream and toasted pecans on top, it is wonderful and not difficult to make. A great dessert choice to elevate your summertime backyard entertaining.

Butter Pecan — Served With Chantilly Cream

Crust

2 cups graham cracker crumbs

½ cup sugar

½ cup finely chopped toasted pecans

1 stick butter, melted

- Combine all dry ingredients in a bowl
- Pour melted butter over dry ingredients
- Mix together until all ingredients are combined
- Using your hands, press mixture evenly into the bottom of a 10 inch spring form pan
- Place spring form pan on top of a cookie sheet or pizza pan - this will prevent butter from dripping onto your oven
- Set aside

Batter

3 – 8 ounces packages cream cheese

2 cups sour cream

1 – 14 ounce can sweetened condensed milk

1 tablespoon vanilla extract

1 teaspoon maple extract

½ cup dark brown sugar

4 large eggs

½ cup toasted chopped pecans

- Preheat oven to 350 degrees
- Using at least a 10 cup capacity food processor, place all ingredients EXCEPT eggs and pecans into the work bowl
- Process on high for about 1-2 minutes or until batter is smooth and lump free
- While still processing the mixture, start adding the eggs - one at a time
- Please know that to achieve best results, you will need to stop processing, remove top of machine, and using a spatula, scrape down the sides of the work bowl and check for lumps
- Continue to process mixture until it is smooth and free of lumps
- Once you are lump free, add the pecans and pulse 2 or 3 times just until pecans are evenly distributed throughout the batter – do not over process – you want to have small pieces of pecans
- Pour batter on top of crust
- Bake for about 1 hour or until you notice that the edges of the cake have risen slightly and are golden brown
- Remove pan from oven and let sit until it is room temperature (about 1½ - 2 hours)
- Place in refrigerator while still in spring form pan for several hours or overnight

Topping

4 ounces cream cheese

⅓ cup powdered sugar

1 teaspoon vanilla extract

¼ teaspoon maple extract

1 cup heavy whipping cream

- Put cream cheese, powdered sugar, vanilla extract and maple extract in a 1 quart mixing bowl
- Using a hand mixer, whip on high until smooth
- Add heavy whipping cream and whip on high until stiff peaks form

To Serve

½ cup of toasted roughly chopped pecans

- Remove cheesecake from spring form pan and transfer to platter
- Spread Chantilly Cream evenly on top of cake
- Sprinkle the top with the toasted pecans

Of all the cheesecakes that I make, the pineapple is the most requested by my children. The sweet, tropical pineapple topping is balanced by the creamy cake. It is nice all year long, and is especially nice when you share it with the ones you love.

Pineapple
Served With Pineapple Topping

Crust

2 cups graham cracker crumbs
½ cup sugar
1 stick butter, melted

- Combine all dry ingredients in a bowl
- Pour melted butter over dry ingredients
- Mix together until all ingredients are combined
- Using your hands, press mixture evenly into the bottom of a 10 inch spring form pan
- Place spring form pan on top of a cookie sheet or pizza pan - this will prevent butter from dripping onto your oven
- Set aside

Batter

3 – 8 ounces packages cream cheese
2 cups sour cream
1 – 14 ounce can sweetened condensed milk
1 tablespoon vanilla extract
4 large eggs

- Preheat oven to 350 degrees
- Using at least a 10 cup capacity food processor, place all ingredients EXCEPT eggs into the work bowl
- Process on high for about 1-2 minutes or until batter is smooth and lump free
- While still processing mixture, start adding the eggs - one at a time
- Please know that to achieve best results, you will need to stop processing, remove top of machine, and using a spatula, scrape down the sides of the work bowl and check for lumps
- Continue to process mixture until it is smooth and free of lumps
- Pour batter on top of crust
- Bake for at least 1 hour or until you notice that the edges of the cake have risen slightly and are golden brown
- Remove pan from oven and let sit until it is room temperature (about 1½ - 2 hours)
- While cake is cooling, prepare topping, see directions below
- Pour warm pineapple topping over cake and let sit until topping is room temperature
- Place in refrigerator while still in spring form pan for several hours or overnight

Topping

1 – 20 ounce can crushed pineapple
¾ cup sugar
3 tablespoons cornstarch
Yellow food coloring (optional)

- Place all ingredients (including the pineapple juice) into a medium sized sauce pan and cook over medium heat stirring often until bubbly and thick
- You may add a few drops of yellow food coloring to enhance the presentation

To Serve

2-3 Kiwi (optional)

- Remove cheesecake from spring form pan and transfer to platter
- Spread Pineapple mixture evenly on top of cake
- If desired, peel, slice and quarter kiwi to decorate cake

The best time to make this cheesecake is when the peaches are ripest, usually during the long, dog days of summer. Nothing says summer more than fresh, juicy peach slices atop the cool, creamy whipped Chantilly topping. There is an added surprise though – slice into the cake and you will find more peaches tucked away in the middle.

Peaches & Cream Served With Chantilly Cream

Crust

2 cups graham cracker crumbs
½ cup sugar
1 stick butter, melted

- Combine all dry ingredients in a bowl
- Pour melted butter over dry ingredients
- Mix together until all ingredients are combined
- Using your hands, press mixture evenly into the bottom of a 10 inch spring form pan
- Place spring form pan on top of a cookie sheet or pizza pan - this will prevent butter from dripping onto your oven
- Set aside

Batter

1 small package (3 ounces) peach gelatin
½ cup water
3 – 8 ounces packages cream cheese
2 cups sour cream
1 – 14 ounce can sweetened condensed milk
1 tablespoon vanilla extract
4 large eggs
1 can (21 ounces) peach pie filling

- Preheat oven to 350 degrees
- Place ½ cup water into a small sauce pan and bring to a boil
- Add the gelatin to the boiling water, remove pan from heat, stir constantly until gelatin is completely dissolved – set aside (Note: gelatin mixture needs to stay liquid, if it sits too long it may congeal in which case you will need to reheat slightly to return it to a liquid form)
- Using at least a 10 cup capacity food processor, place all remaining ingredients EXCEPT eggs, pie filling and gelatin mixture into the work bowl
- Process on high for about 1-2 minutes or until batter is smooth and lump free
- While still processing mixture, start adding the eggs - one at a time
- Please know that to achieve best results, you will need to stop processing, remove top of machine, and using a spatula, scrape down the sides of the work bowl and check for lumps
- Continue to process mixture until it is smooth and free of lumps
- Add the gelatin mixture to the batter and process just until combined – do not over mix – this batter will be a light peach color.
- Pour two-thirds of the batter on top of the crust then carefully spoon peach pie filling over the top
- Pour the remaining batter on top of the peach pie filling
- Bake for about 1 hour or until you notice that the edges of the cake have risen slightly and are golden brown
- Remove pan from oven and let sit until it is room temperature (about 1½ - 2 hours)
- Place in refrigerator while still in spring form pan for several hours or overnight

Topping

4 ounces cream cheese
⅓ cup powdered sugar
1 teaspoon vanilla extract
1 cup heavy whipping cream

- Put cream cheese, powdered sugar, and vanilla extract in a 1 quart mixing bowl
- Using a hand mixer, whip on high until smooth
- Add heavy whipping cream and whip on high until stiff peaks form

To Serve

Fresh, sliced peaches

- Remove cheesecake from spring form pan and transfer to platter
- Swirl Chantilly Cream evenly on top of cake
- Arrange peach slices in a decorative pattern on top

Chocolate, Chocolate & More Chocolate

This cheesecake is for the true chocolate lover. It is full of white chocolate, milk chocolate and semi-sweet chocolate pieces. I think there is probably more chocolate than cheesecake which is perfect for the family member or friend that's a registered chocoholic.

Triple Chocolate Chip

Crust

2 cups graham cracker crumbs
½ cup sugar
1 stick butter, melted

- Combine all dry ingredients in a bowl
- Pour melted butter over dry ingredients
- Mix together until all ingredients are combined
- Using your hands, press mixture evenly into the bottom of a 10 inch spring form pan
- Place spring form pan on top of a cookie sheet or pizza pan - this will prevent butter from dripping onto your oven
- Set aside

Batter

3 – 8 ounces packages cream cheese
2 cups sour cream
1 – 14 ounce can sweetened condensed milk
1 tablespoon vanilla extract
4 large eggs
1 cup semi-sweet chocolate chips
1 cup white chocolate chips
1 cup milk chocolate chips

- Preheat oven to 350 degrees
- Using at least a 10 cup capacity food processor, place all ingredients EXCEPT eggs and all chocolate chips into the work bowl
- Process on high for about 1-2 minutes or until the batter is smooth and lump free
- While still processing mixture, start adding the eggs - one at a time
- Please know that to achieve best results, you will need to stop processing, remove top of machine, and using a spatula, scrape down the sides of the work bowl and check for lumps
- Continue to process mixture until it is smooth and free of lumps
- Once mixture is smooth, add all of the chocolate chips and pulse several times until incorporated
- Pour batter on top of crust
- Bake for at least 1 hour or until you notice that the edges of the cake have risen slightly and are golden brown
- Remove pan from oven and let sit until it is room temperature (about 1½ - 2 hours)
- Place in refrigerator while still in spring form pan for several hours or overnight

To Serve

⅓ cup semi-sweet chocolate chips
⅓ cup white chocolate chips
⅓ cup milk chocolate chips

- Remove cheesecake from spring form pan and transfer to platter
- Place chocolate chips in three separate microwavable bowls (I use small coffee cups)
- Heat the semi-sweet chocolate chips first using 15 second intervals in the microwave – stirring after each interval until chips are melted and smooth – use a spoon or fork to quickly drizzle chocolate over the top of the cake in thin, long streaks
- Repeat this process with the milk chocolate next and the white chocolate last

This dessert is perfect for a more sophisticated palate. The espresso enhances the bold, rich flavor of the chocolate, and the chocolate curl (see directions on next page) adds to the artful presentation. Serve this one with a nice cup of hot coffee, an espresso or perhaps with a brandy.

Espresso with a Chocolate Swirl

Served With Chantilly Cream & Chocolate Drizzle

Crust

2 cups graham cracker crumbs

½ cup sugar

1 stick butter, melted

- Combine all dry ingredients in a bowl
- Pour melted butter over dry ingredients
- Mix together until all ingredients are combined
- Using your hands, press mixture evenly into the bottom of a 10 inch spring form pan
- Place spring form pan on top of a cookie sheet or pizza pan - this will prevent butter from dripping onto your oven
- Set aside

Batter

3 – 8 ounces packages cream cheese

2 cups sour cream

1 – 14 ounce can sweetened condensed milk

1 tablespoon vanilla extract

2 tablespoons espresso powder

¼ cup unsweetened cocoa powder

4 large eggs

- Preheat oven to 350 degrees
- Using at least a 10 cup capacity food processor, place all ingredients EXCEPT unsweetened cocoa powder and eggs into the work bowl
- Process on high for about 1-2 minutes or until batter is smooth and lump free
- While still processing mixture, start adding the eggs - one at a time
- Please know that to achieve best results, you will need to stop processing, remove top of machine, and using a spatula, scrape down the sides of the work bowl and check for lumps
- Continue to process mixture until it is smooth and free of lumps
- Pour half of the batter on top of the crust
- Return work bowl to processor and add the cocoa powder to the remaining batter and process just until combined – do not over process
- Pour this batter on top of the first layer in a circular motion to create a swirl pattern
- Bake for about 1 hour or until you notice that the edges of the cake have risen slightly and are golden brown
- Remove pan from oven and let sit until it is room temperature (about 1½ - 2 hours)
- Place in refrigerator while still in spring form pan for several hours or overnight

Topping

4 ounces cream cheese

⅓ cup powdered sugar

1 teaspoon vanilla extract

1 cup heavy whipping cream

- Put cream cheese, powdered sugar and vanilla extract in a 1 quart mixing bowl
- Using a hand mixer, whip on high until smooth
- Add heavy whipping cream and whip on high until stiff peaks form

Recipe continues on next page...

Espresso with a Chocolate Swirl

**Served With Chantilly Cream
& Chocolate Drizzle**

Continued from the previous page.

To Serve

- Remove cheesecake from spring form pan and transfer to platter
- Spread Chantilly Cream evenly on top of cake

Presentation Options

Chocolate Drizzle

Put ⅓ cup semi-sweet chocolate chips in a small microwaveable container (coffee cup works well) and microwave on medium high heat in 15 second intervals – stirring after each interval – until your chocolate is smooth and melted (do not overcook or chocolate will become dry and hard) then dip a fork or spoon into your melted chocolate and swiftly drizzle over entire cake.

Chocolate Curl

Scatter 1 cup of semi-sweet chocolate chips on a cookie sheet and place in a warm oven (200 degrees) for about 5 minutes or until chips have melted then remove from oven and using a butter knife (or the back of a spoon) spread the melted chips to make a thin layer then allow to cool (I put mine in the refrigerator for a few minutes) using the back of a small metal spatula, scrape the chocolate to make a curl.

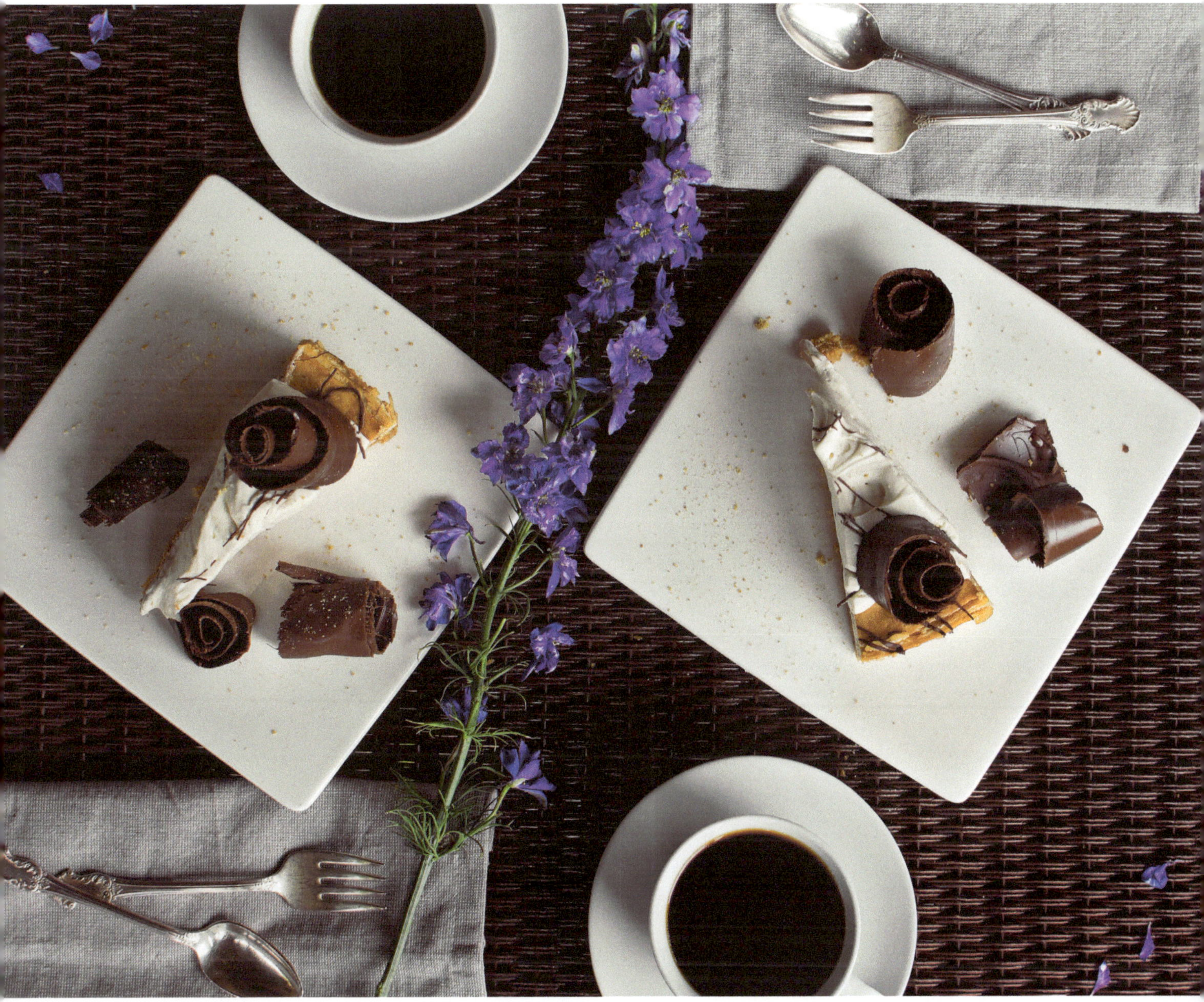

It seems like very few people enjoy a chocolate malted anymore. I personally haven't had one in many, many years. Times have changed, and we no longer have the local malt shops or the drugstore soda fountains. Sometimes it is nice to go back in time to visit and reminisce as well as taste the past. This cheesecake revives that old fashioned, chocolate malted memory. Pull out your poodle skirt and bobbie socks, grab your sweetie and 2 forks and enjoy! Sitting in a 1955 Bel Air convertible is optional.

Chocolate Malted
Served With Malted Chantilly Cream

Crust

2 cups chocolate graham cracker crumbs

½ cup sugar

1 stick butter, melted

- Combine all dry ingredients in a bowl
- Pour melted butter over dry ingredients
- Mix together until all ingredients are combined
- Using your hands, press mixture evenly into the bottom of a 10 inch spring form pan
- Place spring form pan on top of a cookie sheet or pizza pan - this will prevent butter from dripping onto your oven
- Set aside

Batter

3 – 8 ounces packages cream cheese

2 cups sour cream

1 – 14 ounce can sweetened condensed milk

1 tablespoon vanilla extract

5 large eggs

½ cup of malt powder

¼ cup unsweetened cocoa powder

- Preheat oven to 350 degrees
- Using at least a 10 cup capacity food processor, place all ingredients EXCEPT eggs, malt powder and cocoa powder into the work bowl
- Process on high for about 1-2 minutes or until batter is smooth and lump free
- While still processing mixture, start adding the eggs - one at a time
- Please know that to achieve best results, you will need to stop processing, remove top of machine, and using a spatula, scrape down the sides of the work bowl and check for lumps
- Continue to process mixture until it is smooth and free of lumps
- Once you are lump free, add the malt powder and the cocoa powder and process until thoroughly combined
- Pour batter on top of crust
- Bake for about 1 hour or until you notice that the edges of the cake have risen slightly and are golden brown
- Remove pan from oven and let sit until it is room temperature (about 1½ - 2 hours)
- Place in refrigerator while still in spring form pan for several hours or overnight

Topping

4 ounces cream cheese

⅓ cup powdered sugar

1 teaspoon vanilla extract

1 tablespoon malt powder

1 cup heavy whipping cream

- Put cream cheese, powdered sugar, vanilla extract and malt powder in a 1 quart mixing bowl
- Using a hand mixer, whip on high until smooth
- Add heavy whipping cream and whip on high until stiff peaks form

To Serve

Malted milk balls (optional)

- Remove cheesecake from spring form pan and transfer to platter
- Dollop Malted Chantilly Cream on top of cake
- Sprinkle crushed and whole malted milk balls over the top of the Malted Chantilly Cream

Everyone enjoys a really good chocolate chip cookie, and I have been making these cookies for decades. So why not combine the best cookies with the best cheesecake? This variation is one of my favorites, and it's a particular hit with kids and teenagers. Not only do I put chunks of cookies in the batter, I also put chocolate ganache over the entire cake and crumble more cookies on top. I think Cookie Monster would even approve.

Chocolate Chip Cookie

Served With Chocolate Ganache

Crust

2 cups graham cracker crumbs
½ cup sugar
1 stick butter, melted

- Combine all dry ingredients in a bowl
- Pour melted butter over dry ingredients
- Mix together until all ingredients are combined
- Using your hands, press mixture evenly into the bottom of a 10 inch spring form pan
- Place spring form pan on top of a cookie sheet or pizza pan - this will prevent butter from dripping onto your oven
- Set aside

Batter

3 – 8 ounces packages cream cheese
2 cups sour cream
1 – 14 ounce can sweetened condensed milk
1 tablespoon vanilla extract
4 large eggs
5 or 6 chocolate chip cookies

- Preheat oven to 350 degrees
- Using at least a 10 cup capacity food processor, place all ingredients EXCEPT eggs and cookies into the work bowl
- Process on high for about 1-2 minutes or until batter is smooth and lump free
- While still processing mixture, start adding the eggs - one at a time
- Please know that to achieve best results, you will need to stop processing, remove top of machine, and using a spatula, scrape down the sides of the work bowl and check for lumps
- Continue to process mixture until it is smooth and free of lumps
- Crumble cookies into chunks and add to the batter – pulse gently (2 or 3 times) until evenly distributed
- Pour batter on top of crust
- Bake for about 1 hour or until you notice that the edges of the cake have risen slightly and are golden brown
- Remove pan from oven and let sit until it is room temperature (about 1½ - 2 hours)
- Place in refrigerator while still in spring form pan for several hours or overnight

Topping

⅓ cup evaporated milk or heavy cream
1 tablespoon butter
1 cup semi-sweet chocolate chips

- Remove cheesecake from spring form pan and transfer to platter
- Using a small sauce pan, heat milk or cream and butter over medium heat until hot but not boiling
- Remove from heat and add chocolate chips – whisk until chocolate has melted and is smooth
- Immediately pour chocolate ganache over cheesecake and spread evenly

To Serve

5 – 6 chocolate chip cookies, *recipe on following page*

- Roughly chop cookies and sprinkle on top of the chocolate ganache while it is still warm
- You can serve immediately

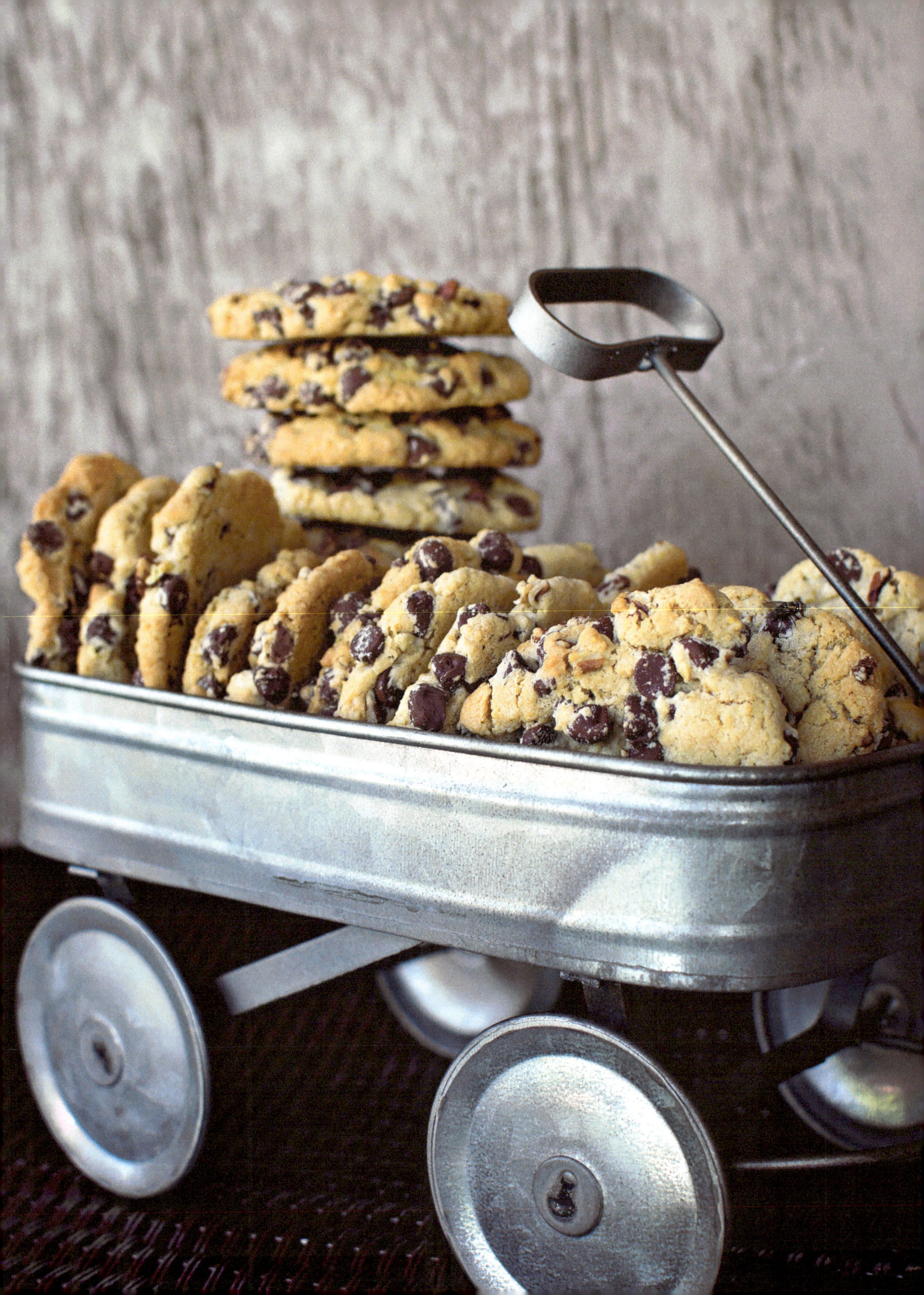

Recipe For Chocolate Chip Cookies

Ingredients

- 1 stick salted butter (room temperature)
- ½ stick butter flavored Crisco (room temperature)
- 1 cup sugar
- ½ cup light brown sugar
- ½ cup dark brown sugar
- 2 large eggs (room temperature)
- 1 tablespoon vanilla
- 2 cups all-purpose flour
- 1 teaspoon salt
- 1 teaspoon baking soda
- 1 ½ teaspoons baking powder
- 2 cups oat flour (see below)
- 1 cup chopped pecans or walnuts *(optional)*
- 4 cups semi-sweet chocolate chips

- Preheat oven to 375 degrees
- Using a stand mixer or hand held mixer (I use a stand mixer) blend butter, Crisco and sugars together
- Add eggs and vanilla and mix until fluffy
- In a separate bowl combine the all-purpose flour, salt, baking soda, and baking powder – mix together
- Add the flour mixture in small batches to the butter mixture – stir until combined
- Add the oat flour in small batches to the dough – stir until combined
- I incorporate the nuts and chocolate chips using a large wooden spoon. This allows me to scrape the bottom of the mixing bowl to evenly distribute the chocolate.
- Drop golf ball size dough onto an ungreased cookie sheet. *Note: you can also use a Silpat sheet or a parchment lined cookie sheet*
- Bake in the middle of the oven for 12 – 15 minutes or until cookies are golden brown around the edges
- Remove from oven, let sit on cookie sheet 10 – 15 minutes before transferring to tray
- This should yield about 3 dozen cookies

- *Note: How to make oat flour - if you have a food processor that is preferable simply put 4 cups of oatmeal (old fashioned or quick cook) into the processor and pulse a minute or so until it has a course texture similar to cornmeal. If you are using a blender the process takes a little longer because you have to do small batches to get the result you desire. Starting with 4 cups of oatmeal may make more than 2 cups of the needed oat flour for the recipe – be sure to measure after this process.*

The best part of the traditional German Chocolate layer cake is the frosting! That's right, the frosting is the star of this dessert. You will love the rich coconut pecan frosting that crowns this luscious cake. When making this cheesecake, I find myself leaving just a little frosting in the pan to enjoy in the privacy of my own kitchen.

German Chocolate
Served With Coconut Pecan Topping

Crust

2 cups graham cracker crumbs
½ cup sugar
1 stick butter, melted

- Combine all dry ingredients in a bowl
- Pour melted butter over dry ingredients
- Mix together until all ingredients are combined
- Using your hands, press mixture evenly into the bottom of a 10 inch spring form pan
- Place spring form pan on top of a cookie sheet or pizza pan - this will prevent butter from dripping onto your oven
- Set aside

Batter

1-4 ounce bar German chocolate
1 cup strong, hot coffee
3 – 8 ounces packages cream cheese
2 cups sour cream
1 – 14 ounce can sweetened condensed milk
1 tablespoon vanilla extract
5 large eggs

- Preheat oven to 350 degrees
- Break up the bar of German chocolate and add it to the cup of strong, hot coffee and set aside – stir after letting it sit for a few minutes in order to allow the chocolate to start melting
- Using at least a 10 cup capacity food processor, place all ingredients EXCEPT the hot coffee/chocolate mixture and eggs into the work bowl
- Process on high for about 1-2 minutes or until batter is smooth and lump free
- While still processing mixture, start adding the eggs - one at a time
- Please know that to achieve best results, you will need to stop processing, remove top of machine, and using a spatula, scrape down the sides of the work bowl and check for lumps
- Continue to process batter until it is smooth and free of lumps
- While you are still processing, slowly add the coffee/chocolate mixture to the batter
- Continue processing until you have a smooth batter (you may need to scrape the sides of the work bowl again to incorporate)
- Pour batter on top of crust
- Bake for about 1 hour or until you notice that the edges of the cake have risen slightly and are golden brown
- Just before cake is ready to come out of the oven, prepare topping, see recipe below
- Remove pan from oven, pour warm coconut pecan topping over cake, and let sit until it is room temperature (about 1½ - 2 hours)
- Place in refrigerator while still in spring form pan for several hours or overnight

Topping

¾ cup evaporated milk (6 oz)
¾ cup sugar
2 egg yolks
1 stick of butter (chopped)
1 teaspoon vanilla extract
1 cup chopped pecans
2 cups flaked coconut

- In a medium sized saucepan over medium high heat cook together evaporated milk, sugar, egg yolks and chopped butter, stirring often until mixture is a golden brown (about 10 – 15 minutes) mixture will be bubbly throughout
- Remove from heat and add vanilla extract, pecans and coconut – stir together

To Serve

- Remove cheesecake from spring form pan and transfer to platter
- Spread Coconut Pecan mixture while it is still warm evenly on top of cake

Who doesn't love a peanut butter cup? It is probably one of the most desired treats at Halloween, Easter or any other holiday for that matter. It had to find its way into one of my cheesecakes, and I knew immediately that it would be a total favorite with kids of all ages.

Peanut Butter Cup   **Served With Chocolate Ganache**

Crust

2 cups graham cracker crumbs

½ cup sugar

1 stick butter, melted

- Combine all dry ingredients in a bowl
- Pour melted butter over dry ingredients
- Mix together until all ingredients are combined
- Using your hands, press mixture evenly into the bottom of a 10 inch spring form pan
- Place spring form pan on top of a cookie sheet or pizza pan - this will prevent butter from dripping onto your oven
- Set aside

Batter

3 – 8 ounces packages cream cheese

2 cups sour cream

1 – 14 ounce can sweetened condensed milk

1 tablespoon vanilla extract

5 large eggs

½ cup peanut butter (smooth or crunchy)

1 cup chopped peanut butter cups

- Preheat oven to 350 degrees
- Using at least a 10 cup capacity food processor, place all ingredients EXCEPT eggs, peanut butter and peanut butter cups into the work bowl
- Process on high for about 1-2 minutes or until batter is smooth and lump free
- While still processing mixture, start adding the eggs (4 of the 5) - one at a time
- Please know that to achieve best results, you will need to stop processing, remove top of machine, and using a spatula, scrape down the sides of the work bowl and check for lumps
- Continue to process mixture until it is smooth and free of lumps
- Pour about half of this batter on top of the crust
- To the remaining mixture, add the peanut butter and the last egg
- Process until smooth and well incorporated – this mixture will be very thick
- Add chopped peanut butter cups to the batter and pulse gently
- This batter may not pour easily, use a spoon or spatula to spread over first layer
- Bake for about 1 hour or until you notice that the edges of the cake have risen slightly and are golden brown
- Remove pan from oven and let sit until it is room temperature (about 1½ - 2 hours)
- Place in refrigerator while still in spring form pan for several hours or overnight

Topping

⅓ cup evaporated milk or heavy cream

1 tablespoon butter

1 cup semi-sweet chocolate chips

- Remove cheesecake from spring form pan and transfer to platter
- Using a small sauce pan heat milk or cream and butter over medium heat until hot but not boiling
- Remove from heat and add chocolate chips – whisk until chocolate has melted and is smooth
- Immediately pour chocolate ganache over cheesecake and spread evenly

To Serve

1-2 cups chopped peanut butter cups

- Sprinkle the chopped peanut butter cups over the warm chocolate ganache

Special Occasion & Seasonal

The Banana Rum Cheesecake is rich with flavors of butterscotch, banana and rum. The cheesecake has subtle flavors and can stand alone or be served with a dollop of whipped cream. Taking this cheesecake to the next level is the warm, butterscotch sauce which is absolutely divine. This sauce, along with the additional rum and fresh bananas, is well worth the extra time and effort!

Banana Rum
Served With Butterscotch Rum Sauce

Crust

2 cups vanilla wafer crumbs or graham cracker crumbs

½ cup sugar

1 stick butter, melted

- Combine all dry ingredients in a bowl
- Pour melted butter over dry ingredients
- Mix together until all ingredients are combined
- Using your hands, press mixture evenly into the bottom of a 10 inch spring form pan
- Place spring form pan on top of a cookie sheet or pizza pan - this will prevent butter from dripping onto your oven
- Set aside

Batter

3 – 8 ounces packages cream cheese

2 cups sour cream

1 – 14 ounce can sweetened condensed milk

1 tablespoon vanilla extract

2 teaspoons rum extract

4 large eggs

2 large bananas mashed

- Preheat oven to 350 degrees
- Using at least a 10 cup capacity food processor, place all ingredients EXCEPT eggs and bananas into the work bowl
- Process on high for about 1-2 minutes
- While still processing the mixture, start adding the eggs - one at a time
- Please know that to achieve best results, you will need to stop processing, remove top of machine, and using a spatula, scrape down the sides of the work bowl and check for lumps throughout the mixing process
- Continue to process mixture until it is smooth and free of lumps
- Once batter is smooth, add mashed bananas and pulse several times
- Pour batter on top of crust
- Bake for at least 1 hour or until you notice that the edges of the cake have risen slightly and are golden brown
- After baking, remove pan from oven and let sit until it is room temperature (about 1½ - 2 hours)
- Then place in refrigerator while still in spring form pan for several hours or overnight

Sauce

1 cup light brown sugar

3 tablespoons light corn syrup

3 tablespoons butter

1 cup heavy cream

½ teaspoon rum extract

2 tablespoons dark rum *(optional)*

3-4 large bananas

- Heat brown sugar, corn syrup and butter in a small sauce pan over medium high heat until butter has melted
- Add cream and slowly bring to a boil - once it reaches a rolling boil, remove from heat and add rum extract and dark rum (if desired) - stir to combine
- Add sliced bananas to sauce while it is still warm

To Serve

- Remove cheesecake from spring form pan and transfer to platter
- For best results, do not pour sauce over entire cake, instead pour sauce over individually sliced pieces. Sauce should be slightly warm or room temperature when serving.

This idea came to me one day as I was enjoying a slice of Black Forest Layer Cake – milk chocolate cake layered with cherries and sweet whipped cream – it was wonderful! I went into my kitchen and designed this cheesecake to replicate the memories of the traditional Black Forest layer cake. I was pleased with the results, and I hope you will be as well.

Black Forest   **Served With Cherry's Jubilee**

Crust

2 cups chocolate graham cracker crumbs

½ cup sugar

1 stick butter, melted

- Combine all dry ingredients in a bowl
- Pour melted butter over dry ingredients
- Mix together until all ingredients are combined
- Using your hands, press mixture evenly into the bottom of a 10 inch spring form pan
- Place spring form pan on top of a cookie sheet or pizza pan - this will prevent butter from dripping onto your oven
- Set aside

Batter

3 – 8 ounces packages cream cheese

2 cups sour cream

1 – 14 ounce can sweetened condensed milk

1 tablespoon vanilla extract

5 large eggs

1 tablespoon instant coffee

½ cup unsweetened cocoa powder

- Preheat oven to 350 degrees
- Using at least a 10 cup capacity food processor place all ingredients EXCEPT eggs, instant coffee and cocoa powder into the work bowl
- Process on high for about 1-2 minutes or until batter is smooth and lump free
- White still processing mixture, start adding the eggs - one at a time
- Please know that to achieve best results, you will need to stop processing, remove top of machine, and using a spatula, scrape down the sides of the work bowl and check for lumps throughout the mixing process
- Continue to process mixture until it is smooth and free of lumps
- While you are still processing, add the instant coffee and cocoa powder to the mixture continue processing until you have a smooth batter
- Pour batter on top of the crust
- Bake for at least 1 hour or until you notice that the edges of the cake have risen slightly and are golden brown
- Remove pan from oven and let sit until it is room temperature (about 1½ - 2 hours)
- Place in refrigerator while still in spring form pan for several hours or overnight

Topping

1 – 14 ounce can sour, pitted cherries (juice included)

1 – 15 ounce can dark, sweet, pitted cherries (juice included)

½ teaspoon salt

3 tablespoons cornstarch

1 cup sugar

1- 20 ounce can cherry pie filling

- In a medium sized saucepan, add all the ingredients EXCEPT the cherry pie filling and cook over medium heat, stirring occasionally – make sure the cornstarch is dissolved
- Bring mixture to a rolling boil (continue to stir), once it becomes very thick remove from heat and add the cherry pie filling
- Pour about half of the topping over your cold cheesecake while it is still in the spring form pan – reserve the remainder of the topping to use for serving

To Serve

- Remove cheesecake from spring form pan and transfer to platter
- Serve each piece with additional topping on the side if desired

A good friend of mine, George, owner of a wonderful restaurant here in my hometown, had mentioned to me that he had tasted this combination once in a restaurant in France where he grew up. He wondered if I was interested in the challenge of trying to make one. I love a challenge, but I was very skeptical. The idea of incorporating blue cheese into a dessert cheesecake did not seem appealing to me at first. It took me a while to conjure up the nerve to try to make this combination work. After much experimentation, I was surprisingly delighted with the results: savory and sweet. Thank you George for this inspiration!

Blue Pear — Served With Chantilly Cream

Crust

2 cups graham cracker crumbs
½ cup sugar
½ cup finely chopped English walnuts
1 stick butter, melted

- Combine all dry ingredients in a bowl
- Pour melted butter over dry ingredients
- Mix together until all ingredients are combined
- Using your hands, press mixture evenly into the bottom of a 10 inch spring form pan
- Place spring form pan on top of a cookie sheet or pizza pan - this will prevent butter from dripping onto your oven
- Set aside

Batter

3 – 8 ounces packages cream cheese
2 cups sour cream
1 – 14 ounce can sweetened condensed milk
1 tablespoon vanilla extract
1 teaspoon ground nutmeg
1 – 15 ounce container whole milk ricotta cheese
½ cup crumbled Gorgonzola
1 cup finely chopped dried pears
4 large eggs

- Preheat oven to 350 degrees
- Using at least a 10 cup capacity food processor, place all ingredients EXCEPT ricotta, Gorgonzola, dried pears and eggs into the work bowl
- Process on high for about 1-2 minutes or until the batter is smooth and lump free
- While still processing mixture, start adding the eggs - one at a time
- Please know that to achieve best results, you will need to stop processing, remove top of machine, and using a spatula, scrape down the sides of the work bowl and check for lumps
- Continue to process mixture until it is smooth and free of lumps. Once you are lump free, add the ricotta and process until smooth – do not over process
- Add the dried pear pieces and Gorgonzola and pulse a few times – you want to see small pieces of pear and Gorgonzola throughout your batter
- Pour batter on top of crust
- Bake for about 1 hour or until you notice that the edges of the cake have risen slightly and are golden brown
- Remove pan from oven and let sit until it is room temperature (about 1½ - 2 hours)
- Place in refrigerator while still in spring form pan for several hours or overnight

Topping

4 ounces cream cheese
⅓ cup powdered sugar
1 teaspoon vanilla extract
1 cup heavy whipping cream

- Put cream cheese, powdered sugar and vanilla extract in a 1 quart mixing bowl
- Using a hand mixer, whip on high until smooth
- Add heavy whipping cream and whip on high until stiff peaks form

To Serve

½ cup of finely chopped dried pears
⅛ teaspoon ground nutmeg

- Remove cheesecake from spring form pan and transfer to platter
- Spread Chantilly Cream evenly on top of cake
- Sprinkle the top with the dried pear pieces and ground nutmeg. *Note: nutmeg is a strong spice, use sparingly – less is better*

I love making this cheesecake for several reasons but mostly because it is so colorful and eye-catching. The season when berries are plentiful is the right time to enjoy this one. Most people love berries and cream, so this is a hit every time I serve it. The not-too-sweet cake pairs beautifully with the fresh, mixed berries.

Dazzle Berry

Served With Raspberry Glaze & Chantilly Cream

Crust

2 cups graham cracker crumbs
½ cup sugar
1 stick butter, melted

- Combine all dry ingredients in a bowl
- Pour melted butter over dry ingredients
- Mix together until all ingredients are combined
- Using your hands, press mixture evenly into the bottom of a 10 inch spring form pan
- Place spring form pan on top of a cookie sheet or pizza pan - this will prevent butter from dripping onto your oven
- Set aside

Batter

3 – 8 ounces packages cream cheese
2 cups sour cream
1 – 14 ounce can sweetened condensed milk
1 tablespoon vanilla extract
4 large eggs

- Preheat oven to 350 degrees
- Using at least a 10 cup capacity food processor, place all ingredients EXCEPT eggs into the work bowl
- Process on high for about 1-2 minutes or until batter is smooth and lump free
- While still processing mixture, start adding the eggs - one at a time
- Please know that to achieve best results, you will need to stop processing, remove top of machine, and using a spatula, scrape down the sides of the work bowl and check for lumps
- Continue to process mixture until it is smooth and free of lumps
- Pour batter on top of crust
- Bake for about 1 hour or until you notice that the edges of the cake have risen slightly and are golden brown
- Remove pan from oven and let sit until it is room temperature (about 1½ - 2 hours)
- Place in refrigerator while still in spring form pan for several hours or overnight

Topping

1 cup seedless raspberry jam
4 ounces cream cheese
⅓ cup powdered sugar
1 teaspoon vanilla extract
1 cup heavy whipping cream

- Remove cheesecake from spring form pan and transfer to platter
- Place raspberry jam in a microwavable bowl and heat until spreadable (about 30 seconds)
- Spread raspberry glaze over cake stopping about ½ inch from the outer edge
- Put cream cheese, powdered sugar and vanilla extract in a 1 quart mixing bowl
- Using a hand mixer, whip on high until smooth
- Add heavy whipping cream and whip on high until stiff peaks form

To Serve

Fresh blackberries, raspberries, kiwi, blueberries, strawberries (any combination)

- Spread Chantilly Cream evenly on top of the raspberry glaze going all the way to the edge of the cake - this creates a smooth, white canvas to work with
- Arrange fresh berries in a decorative pattern – make sure berries are completely dry before using

Thanksgiving would not be complete without this treasure. The fragrant gingersnap crust and the spicy swirl of pumpkin will fill your home with the welcoming spirit of the holidays. This is very popular at the restaurant during the Thanksgiving holiday season.

Pumpkin Spice
Served With Spiced Chantilly Cream

Crust

2 cups ginger snap crumbs
½ cup of sugar
1 stick of butter, melted

- Combine all dry ingredients in a bowl
- Pour melted butter over dry ingredients
- Mix together until all ingredients are combined
- Using your hands, press mixture evenly into the bottom of a 10 inch spring form pan
- Place spring form pan on top of a cookie sheet or pizza pan - this will prevent butter from dripping onto your oven
- Set aside

Batter

3 – 8 ounces packages cream cheese
2 cups sour cream
1 – 14 ounce can sweetened condensed milk
1 tablespoon vanilla extract
1 tablespoon pumpkin pie spice
½ teaspoon salt
1-15 ounce can pure pumpkin
½ cup light brown sugar
6 large eggs

- Preheat oven to 350 degrees
- Using at least a 10 cup capacity food processor, place the first four ingredients into the work bowl
- Process on high for about 1-2 minutes or until batter is smooth and lump free
- While still processing mixture, start adding 4 of the 6 eggs - one at a time
- Please know that to achieve best results, you will need to stop processing, remove top of machine, and using a spatula, scrape down the sides of the work bowl and check for lumps
- Continue to process mixture until it is smooth and free of lumps
- Pour half of the batter on top of the crust
- Return container to processor and add to the remaining mixture the pumpkin pie spice, salt, pumpkin, brown sugar and the last 2 eggs
- Process until all ingredients are fully incorporated and mixture is smooth and lump free
- Pour this batter on top of the first layer in a circular motion to create a swirl pattern
- Bake for at least 1 hour or until you notice that the edges of the cake have risen slightly and are golden brown
- Remove pan from oven and let sit until it is room temperature (about 1½ - 2 hours)
- Place in refrigerator while still in spring form pan for several hours or overnight

Topping

4 ounces cream cheese
⅓ cup powdered sugar
1 teaspoon vanilla extract
¼ teaspoon pumpkin pie spice
1 cup heavy whipping cream

- Put cream cheese, powdered sugar, vanilla extract and pumpkin pie spice in a 1 quart mixing bowl
- Using a hand mixer, whip on high until smooth
- Add heavy whipping cream and whip on high until stiff peaks form

To Serve

- Remove cheesecake from spring form pan and transfer to platter
- Swirl Spiced Chantilly Cream topping evenly on top of cake *(optional)*.
- This recipe is also delicious without the Chantilly Cream topping, as in photo at left

I was talked into creating this one for Halloween for my son's restaurant. I sometimes use food coloring to enhance appearance, but I do have a moral compass when it comes to using massive amounts of red food coloring. For this reason, I've added pureed red beets to the batter to ease my soul and to provide the necessary coloring. I have often added candy eyeballs around the raspberry jam to create an ominous and fun display. The candy glass shards further enhance the effect. Happy Halloween!

Dead Velvet — Served With Chantilly Cream & Candy Glass Shards

Crust

2 cups graham cracker crumbs or chocolate graham cracker crumbs

½ cup sugar

½ cup finely chopped pecans

1 stick butter, melted

- Combine all dry ingredients in a bowl
- Pour melted butter over dry ingredients
- Mix together until all ingredients are combined
- Using your hands, press mixture evenly into the bottom of a 10 inch spring form pan
- Place spring form pan on top of a cookie sheet or pizza pan - this will prevent butter from dripping onto your oven
- Set aside

Batter

3 – 8 ounces packages cream cheese

1 cup sour cream

1 – 14 ounce can sweetened condensed milk

1 tablespoon vanilla extract

2 cups whole milk ricotta cheese

½ teaspoon salt

4 large eggs

4 tablespoons unsweetened cocoa powder

1 tablespoon cornstarch

1 cup beet puree (see directions on next page)

Red food coloring *(optional)*

- Preheat oven to 350 degrees
- Using at least a 10 cup capacity food processor, place all ingredients EXCEPT eggs, cocoa powder, cornstarch and beet puree into the work bowl
- Process on high for about 1-2 minutes or until batter is smooth and lump free
- While still processing mixture, start adding the eggs - one at a time
- After the eggs are totally incorporated, add the cocoa powder and cornstarch and process
- Please know that to achieve best results, you will need to stop processing, remove top of machine, and using a spatula, scrape down the sides of the work bowl and check for lumps
- Continue to process mixture until it is smooth and free of lumps
- Once you are lump free, add the beet puree and process until thoroughly combined – do not over process
- You want this batter to have a rich, red color (similar to a red velvet cake). Add red food coloring, one teaspoon at a time – pulsing after each addition until you achieve the desired color
- Pour batter on top of crust
- Bake for at least 1 hour or until you notice that the edges of the cake have risen slightly and are golden brown
- Remove pan from oven and let sit until it is room temperature (about 1½ - 2 hours)
- Then place in refrigerator while still in spring form pan for several hours or overnight

Topping

4 ounces cream cheese

⅓ cup powdered sugar

1 teaspoon vanilla extract

1 cup heavy whipping cream

- Put cream cheese, powdered sugar and vanilla extract in a 1 quart mixing bowl
- Using a hand mixer, whip on high until smooth
- Add heavy whipping cream and whip on high until stiff peaks form

Recipe continues on next page...

Dead Velvet

Served With Chantilly Cream & Candy Glass Shards

Continued from previous page

To Serve

⅓ cup red raspberry jam or preserves

Candy "glass shards" *(optional)* - see recipe below

- Remove cheesecake from spring form pan and transfer to platter
- Spread Chantilly Cream evenly on top of cake
- Put jam or preserves in a small microwavable container and heat for 20 – 30 seconds. Stir briskly it will become very thin and smooth
- Using a small spoon, drop small amounts of the melted jam or preserves over the top of the Chantilly Cream.
- Decorate cake by piercing it with candy "glass shards" (recipe below)

Beet Puree

In a medium sized sauce pan place 2 large (or 3 small), red beets that have been cleaned, peeled and quartered along with ½ cup sugar, ¼ cup water, and ½ teaspoon salt. Cover and simmer over medium low temperature until tender (approximately 20 minutes). Once beets are tender, remove from heat, and set aside to cool to room temperature. Place beets and any remaining liquid into a blender and puree until smooth. This may make more than 1 cup.

Candy "Glass Shards"

Spray a large cookie sheet with non-stick cooking spray or a small amount of oil - wipe excess away with a paper towel and set aside. In a medium sized sauce pan add 1 cup water, ½ cup light corn syrup, 1¾ cup sugar, and ⅛ teaspoon cream of tarter – quickly stir together then place over medium high heat. Cook, without stirring, until your mixture reaches a roiling boil and the candy thermometer shows 300 degrees (hard crack stage). This will take about 20 minutes – be sure to monitor your candy thermometer closely. Once it reaches this point, pour mixture over the prepared cookie sheet, pick up cookie sheet and tilt the pan to allow mixture to evenly cover the bottom. This must be done quickly to prevent candy from setting up and to ensure a thin layer is created. Set aside to cool (15-20 minutes). Using a butter knife or metal spatula, gently lift the candy from the cookie sheet and break into pieces.

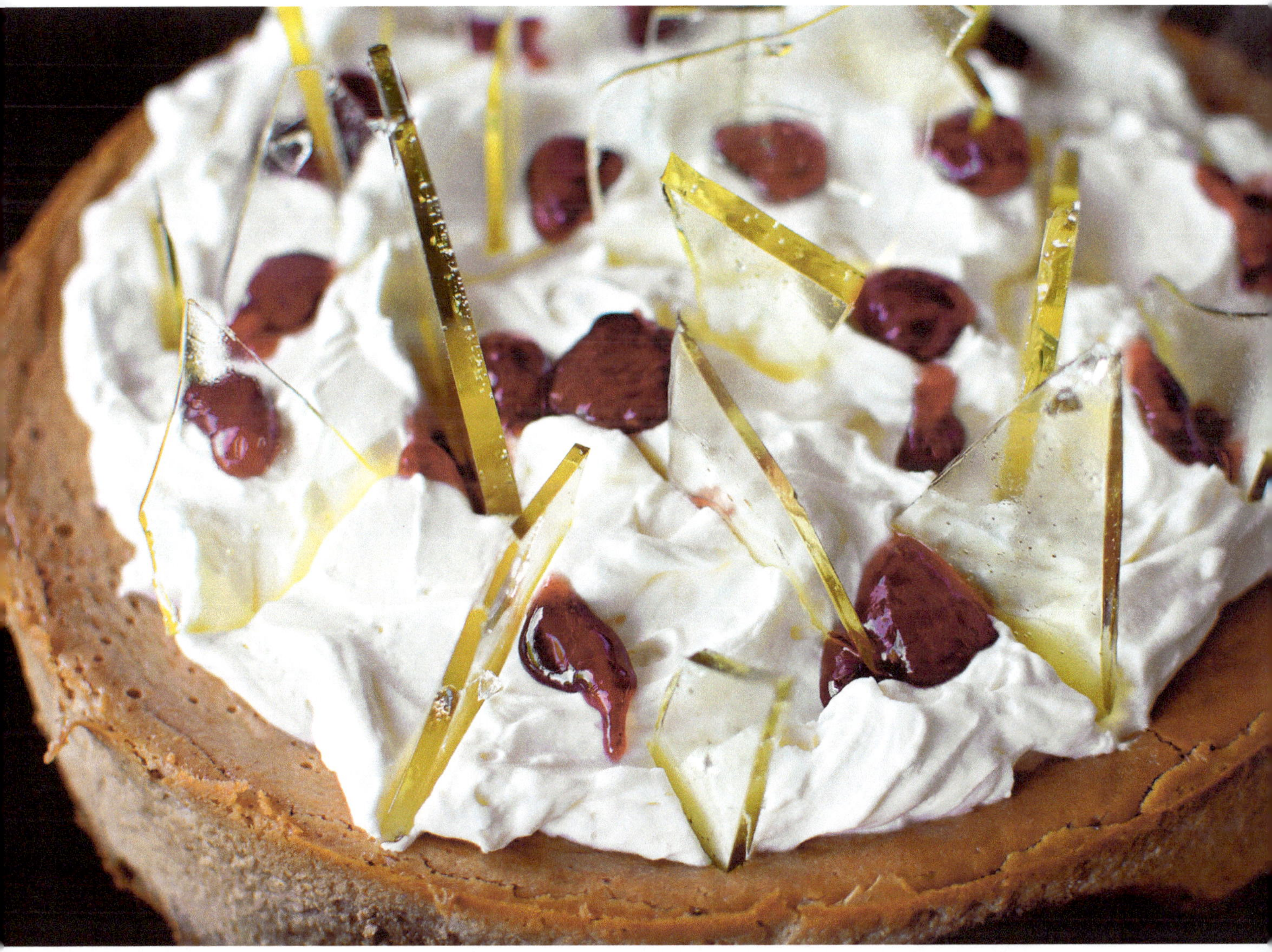

Who doesn't like a good crème brule following a great meal in a nice restaurant? Nothing is better than taking your spoon and breaking through the bruled sugar to get to the real treasure – the light, vanilla custard. You naturally close your eyes when you take that first bite! I tiptoed around this recipe for quite a while before I became satisfied with the final result. Personally, nothing can take the place of a true crème brule, not even my version. But it is quite nice, and my friends love it.

Crème Brule   **Served With Sugar Wafers**

Crust

2 cups graham cracker crumbs

½ cup sugar

1 stick butter, melted

- Combine all dry ingredients in a bowl
- Pour melted butter over dry ingredients
- Mix together until all ingredients are combined
- Using your hands, press mixture evenly into the bottom of a 10 inch spring form pan
- Place spring form pan on top of a cookie sheet or pizza pan - this will prevent butter from dripping onto your oven
- Set aside

Batter

3 – 8 ounces packages cream cheese

2 cups sour cream

1 – 14 ounce can sweetened condensed milk

1 tablespoon vanilla extract

1 teaspoon caramel extract

8 large eggs

1 cup heavy cream

- Preheat oven to 350 degrees
- Using at least a 10 cup capacity food processor, place all ingredients EXCEPT eggs and the heavy cream into the work bowl
- Process on high for about 1-2 minutes or until batter is smooth and lump free
- While still processing mixture, start adding the eggs - one at a time
- Please know that to achieve best results, you will need to stop processing, remove top of machine, and using a spatula, scrape down the sides of the container and check for lumps
- Continue to process mixture until it is smooth and free of lumps
- Add the heavy cream and process until thoroughly combined – this will be a very thin batter
- Pour batter on top of crust
- Bake for about 1 hour or until you notice that the edges of the cake have risen slightly and are golden brown
- Remove pan from oven and let sit until it is room temperature (about 1½ - 2 hours)
- Place in refrigerator while still in spring form pan for several hours or overnight

To Serve

Granulated sugar

Kitchen torch

Sugar Wafers (see directions on next page)

- Remove cheesecake from spring form pan and transfer to platter
- For best results, slice and plate, sprinkle 2 teaspoons of granulated sugar evenly on top of each piece
- Using your kitchen torch, move it back and forth across the top, holding it about 3 or 4 inches away until you achieve a bubbly, amber colored hard shell
- Top with sugar wafers. Serve immediately – I've noticed that if you let it sit too long, the shell becomes liquid

Recipe continues on next page...

Crème Brule

Served With Sugar Wafers

Continued from previous page

Sugar Wafers

Put 1 cup granulated sugar in a non-stick skillet and cook over medium high heat. Using a wooden spoon, constantly stir the sugar until it melts and turns an amber color liquid. Place a Silpat cooking mat on a cookie sheet and with a small spoon or fork, drizzle the melted sugar into your desired pattern or shape. Wafers should be "set" and ready to lift off and use after 10 - 15 minutes.

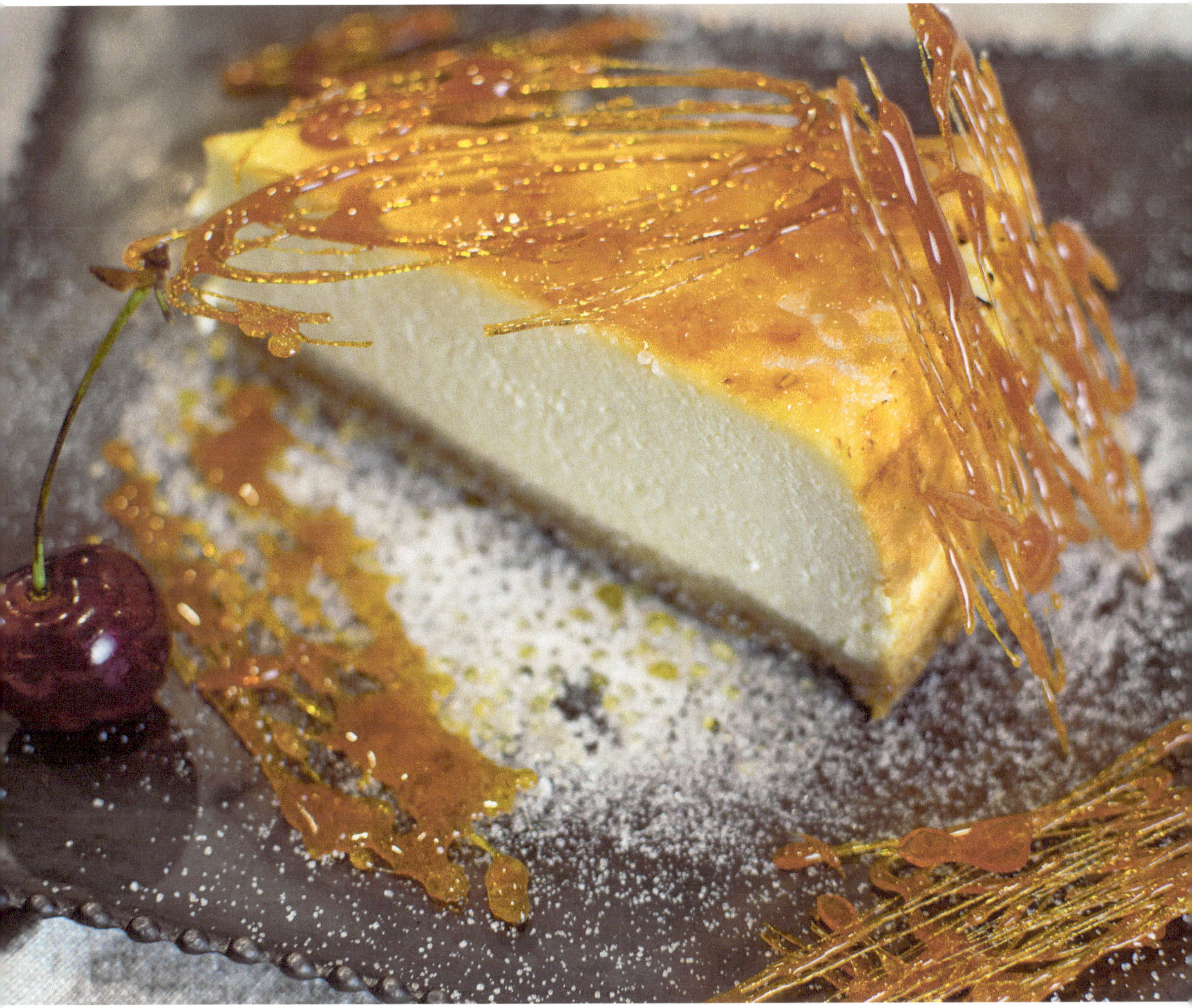

The Eggnog Cheesecake has a very light, smooth texture. With the hint of nutmeg and the gingersnap crust, it is as wonderful to smell it as it is to eat. This cake is good served room temperature or cold. It is a perfect treat to serve family and friends throughout the holiday season. Cheers!

Eggnog

Served With Chantilly Cream

Crust

2 cups ginger snap crumbs
½ cup sugar
1 stick butter, melted

- Combine all dry ingredients in a bowl
- Pour melted butter over dry ingredients
- Mix together until all ingredients are combined
- Using your hands, press mixture evenly into the bottom of a 10 inch spring form pan
- Place spring form pan on top of a cookie sheet or pizza pan - this will prevent butter from dripping onto your oven
- Set aside

Batter

3 – 8 ounces packages cream cheese
2 cups sour cream
1 – 14 ounce can sweetened condensed milk
1 tablespoon vanilla extract
1 teaspoon ground nutmeg
6 large eggs
2 tablespoons corn starch
2 cups of eggnog

- Using at least a 10 cup capacity food processor, place all ingredients EXCEPT eggnog and eggs into the work bowl
- Process on high for about 1-2 minutes or until batter is smooth and lump free
- While still processing mixture, start adding the eggs - one at a time
- Add the cornstarch after the eggs are totally incorporated
- Please know that to achieve best results, you will need to stop processing, remove top of machine, and using a spatula, scrape down the sides of the work bowl and check for lumps
- Continue to process mixture until it is smooth and free of lumps
- Once you are lump free, add the eggnog and process just until combined – do not over process (about 15 seconds)
- This batter will be extremely thin
- Pour batter on top of crust
- Bake for about 1 hour or until you notice that the edges of the cake have risen slightly and are golden brown
- Remove pan from oven and let sit until it is room temperature (about 1½ - 2 hours)
- Place in refrigerator while still in spring form pan for several hours or overnight

Topping

4 ounces cream cheese
⅓ cup powdered sugar
1 teaspoon vanilla extract
1 cup heavy whipping cream

- Put cream cheese, powdered sugar and vanilla extract in a 1 quart mixing bowl
- Using a hand mixer, whip on high until smooth
- Add heavy whipping cream and whip on high until stiff peaks form

To Serve

⅛ teaspoon ground nutmeg

- Remove cheesecake from spring form pan and transfer to platter
- Spread Chantilly Cream evenly on top of cake, optional
- Sprinkle the top with nutmeg *(Note: nutmeg is a strong spice use sparingly – less is better)*
- This recipe is also delicious without the Chantilly Cream topping, as in photo at left

Ask anyone what their favorite part of a wedding is and without hesitation most people will say – the wedding cake, of course. A few years ago my grandson Cade, was telling me about a cupcake his mother had bought at a very popular bakery in Nashville. It tasted just like a heavenly piece of wedding cake. He asked me if I could make a cheesecake that tasted like that cupcake, and I did! This rich vanilla/almond cheesecake is elegant and authentic. I've had many brides serve this cake at their wedding receptions.

Wedding Cake

Crust

2 cups vanilla wafer crumbs
½ cup sugar
1 stick butter, melted

- Combine all dry ingredients in a bowl
- Pour melted butter over dry ingredients
- Mix together until all ingredients are combined
- Using your hands, press mixture evenly into the bottom of a 10 inch spring form pan
- Place spring form pan on top of a cookie sheet or pizza pan - this will prevent butter from dripping onto your oven
- Set aside

Batter

3 – 8 ounces packages cream cheese
2 cups sour cream
1 – 14 ounce can sweetened condensed milk
1 tablespoon vanilla extract
1 teaspoon almond extract
4 large eggs

- Preheat oven to 350 degrees
- Using at least a 10 cup capacity food processor, place all ingredients EXCEPT eggs into the work bowl
- Process on high for about 1-2 minutes or until batter is smooth and lump free
- While still processing mixture, start adding the eggs - one at a time
- Please know that to achieve best results, you will need to stop processing, remove top of machine, and using a spatula, scrape down the sides of the work bowl and check for lumps
- Continue to process mixture until it is smooth and free of lumps
- Pour batter on top of crust
- Bake for at least 1 hour or until you notice that the edges of the cake have risen slightly and are golden brown
- Remove pan from oven and let sit until it is room temperature (about 1½ - 2 hours)
- Place in refrigerator while still in spring form pan for several hours or overnight

Frosting

8 ounces cream cheese (room temperature)
1 stick butter (room temperature)
6 cups powdered sugar
2 teaspoons vanilla extract
1 teaspoon almond extract
⅓ – ½ cup heavy whipping cream

- Put cream cheese, butter, powdered sugar, vanilla and almond extracts in a mixing bowl
- Using a hand mixer or a stand mixer, whip on high until throughly combined (frosting will be very thick)
- While mixing, add the heavy whipping cream 1 tablespoon at a time until you have achieved a smooth, creamy spreadable consistency (you will use at least ⅓ cup)

To Serve

White, edible, decorative pearls

- Remove cheesecake from spring form pan and transfer to platter
- Spread Whipped Cream Cheese Frosting evenly on top and sides of cake
- Sprinkle the top with the edible, decorative pearls

Where there is a bride and a wedding cake, there is also a groom and his special cake. The Groom's Cake Cheesecake features layers of chocolate and vanilla – from the crust to the decoration. I use chocolate ganache and white chocolate bow ties to evoke the feeling of a formal affair. However, you could also choose to have a white chocolate ganache with black bow ties. This is simple yet elegant either way.

Groom's Cake   Served With Chocolate Ganache

Crust

2 cups chocolate graham cracker crumbs

½ cup sugar

1 stick butter, melted

- Combine all dry ingredients in a bowl
- Pour melted butter over dry ingredients
- Mix together until all ingredients are combined
- Using your hands, press mixture evenly into the bottom of a 10 inch spring form pan
- Place spring form pan on top of a cookie sheet or pizza pan - this will prevent butter from dripping onto your oven, set aside

Batter

3 – 8 ounces packages cream cheese

2 cups sour cream

1 – 14 ounce can sweetened condensed milk

1 tablespoon vanilla extract

5 large eggs

⅓ cup unsweetened cocoa powder

2 teaspoons instant coffee powder

- Preheat oven to 350 degrees
- Using at least a 10 cup capacity food processor, place all ingredients EXCEPT eggs, cocoa powder and instant coffee into the work bowl
- Process on high for about 1-2 minutes or until batter is smooth and lump free
- While still processing mixture, start adding the eggs - one at a time
- Please know that to achieve best results, you will need to stop processing, remove top of machine, and using a spatula, scrape down the sides of the work bowl and check for lumps
- Continue to process mixture until it is smooth and free of lumps
- Pour about half of this batter into a large measuring cup or bowl that has a pouring spout
- To the remaining mixture, add the cocoa powder and instant coffee and process until smooth
- Pour this mixture on top of the crust and bake for 20 minutes
- Remove from the oven and very slowly and very gently pour the vanilla batter on top of the chocolate layer. Start at the outside edge and as close to the cake as you can, pour lightly around the cake until the batter floods the center using all of the vanilla batter. *Caution: if you pour directly onto the center of the cake, it will pierce the chocolate layer and you will not have two distinct layers when finished*
- Return to oven and bake for another 40 minutes or until you notice that the edges of the cake have risen slightly and are golden brown
- Remove pan from oven and let sit until it is room temperature (about 1½ - 2 hours)
- Place in refrigerator while still in spring form pan for several hours or overnight

Topping

⅓ cup evaporated milk or heavy cream

1 tablespoon butter

1 cup semi-sweet chocolate chips

- Remove cheesecake from spring form pan and transfer to platter
- Using a small sauce pan heat milk or cream and butter over medium heat until hot but not boiling
- Remove from heat and add chocolate chips – whisk until chocolate has melted and is smooth
- Immediately pour chocolate ganache over cheesecake and spread evenly

To Serve

1 cup white chocolate chips

Bow tie mold pan

- Melt white chocolate chips in the microwave using 15 second intervals, stirring after each interval until smooth. *Caution: white chocolate chips sometimes do not melt smoothly, if this happens, add a tablespoon of coconut oil – this will help thin the chocolate and make it smooth and easy to work with*
- Pour melted chocolate into the bow tie molds, careful not to overfill. You can use a knife to scrape off excess
- Place molds in the refrigerator for about 15 minutes or until hardened
- Pop out bow ties and arrange them on cake

Kids at Heart

One day when I was delivering cheesecakes to my son's restaurant, one of the chef's, Red, asked if I could create a cheesecake with chocolate, strawberry and vanilla layers just like Neapolitan ice cream. I thought about this for days, trying to figure out how to keep the layers from blending together. The only way I could accomplish this was to bake each layer just enough to "set" them before adding the next layer. I repeated this "bake and set" process for each layer. When I sliced it, there it was – three perfect layers. To me, this is so whimsical and fun especially for a party.

Neapolitan
Served With Chantilly Cream

Crust

2 cups chocolate graham cracker crumbs or regular graham cracker crumbs

½ cup sugar

1 stick butter, melted

- Combine all dry ingredients in a bowl
- Pour melted butter over dry ingredients
- Mix together until all ingredients are combined
- Using your hands, press mixture evenly into the bottom of a 10 inch spring form pan
- Place spring form pan on top of a cookie sheet or pizza pan - this will prevent butter from dripping onto your oven, set aside

Batter

3 – 8 ounces packages cream cheese

2 cups sour cream

1 – 14 ounce can sweetened condensed milk

1 tablespoon vanilla extract

4 large eggs

¼ cup unsweetened cocoa powder

1 teaspoon instant coffee

⅓ cup strawberry preserves

2-4 drops of red food coloring

- Preheat oven to 350 degrees
- Using at least a 10 cup capacity food processor, place the first four ingredients into the work bowl
- Process on high for about 1-2 minutes or until batter is smooth and lump free
- While still processing mixture, start adding the eggs - one at a time
- Please know that to achieve best results, you will need to stop processing, remove top of machine, and using a spatula, scrape down the sides of the work bowl and check for lumps
- Continue to process mixture until it is smooth and free of lumps
- Divide batter into 3 equal parts (about 2 cups each) leave 1 part in the food processor and put the other parts into separate measuring bowls or mixing bowls that have a pouring spout – the pouring spout is very important
- To the mixture left in the food processor, add the cocoa powder and the instant coffee – process until smooth and ingredients are incorporated
- Pour the chocolate mixture on top of the chocolate crust and spread evenly
- Bake for about 15 minutes
- Remove from the oven and very slowly and very gently pour the vanilla batter on top of the chocolate layer. Start at the outside edge and as close to the cake as you can pour lightly around the cake until the batter floods the center using all of the vanilla batter. *Caution: if you pour directly onto the center of the cake, it will pierce the chocolate layer and you will not have three distinct layers when finished*
- Return cake to the oven and bake for another 15 minutes
- While this layer is baking, add the preserves and food coloring to the last bowl of batter
- Using a hand mixer, blend thoroughly ensuring that the batter is smooth
- Remove cake from oven and repeat process with the last layer – being sure the pour gently and carefully from the edge
- Return the cake to the oven and continue to bake for 30 minutes - you will notice that the edges of the cake have risen slightly and are golden brown
- Remove pan from oven and let sit until it is room temperature (about 1½ - 2 hours)
- Place in refrigerator while still in spring form pan for several hours or overnight

Topping

4 ounces cream cheese

⅓ cup powdered sugar

1 teaspoon vanilla extract

1 cup heavy whipping cream

- Put cream cheese, powdered sugar and vanilla extract in a 1 quart mixing bowl
- Using a hand mixer, whip on high until smooth
- Add heavy whipping cream and whip on high until stiff peaks form

To Serve

Stemmed maraschino cherries

- Remove cheesecake from spring form pan and transfer to platter
- Dollop Chantilly Cream evenly on top of cake
- Drain cherries on a paper towel until dry and decorate each slice with a stemmed cherry

Orange creamsicles, orange push up pops, and orange cream bars – no matter what you called them as a kid, they were always a treat when the ice cream truck came rolling through your neighborhood. This cake is dense and full of creamy, orange flavor while the Chantilly topping adds a light and fluffy vanilla layer. The mandarin oranges bring a burst of freshness and color. Who needs an ice cream truck when you have this?

Orange Crème Pop — Served With Chantilly Cream

Crust

2 cups graham cracker crumbs

½ cup sugar

1 stick butter, melted

- Combine all dry ingredients in a bowl
- Pour melted butter over dry ingredients
- Mix together until all ingredients are combined
- Using your hands, press mixture evenly into the bottom of a 10 inch spring form pan
- Place spring form pan on top of a cookie sheet or pizza pan - this will prevent butter from dripping onto your oven, set aside

Batter

1 small package (3 ounces) orange gelatin

½ cup water

3 – 8 ounces packages cream cheese

2 cups sour cream

1 – 14 ounce can sweetened condensed milk

1 tablespoon vanilla extract

1 teaspoon orange extract

4 large eggs

- Preheat oven to 350 degrees
- Place ½ cup of water into a small sauce pan and bring to a boil
- Add the gelatin to the boiling water, remove pan from heat, stir constantly until gelatin is completely dissolved. Set aside. *Note: gelatin mixture needs to stay liquid, if it sits too long it may congeal in which case you will need to reheat slightly to return it to a liquid form*
- Using at least a 10 cup capacity food processor, place all remaining ingredients EXCEPT eggs, (and gelatin mixture) into the work bowl
- Process on high for about 1-2 minutes or until batter is smooth and lump free
- While still processing mixture, start adding the eggs - one at a time
- Please know that to achieve best results, you will need to stop processing, remove top of machine, and using a spatula, scrape down the sides of the work bowl and check for lumps
- Continue to process mixture until it is smooth and free of lumps
- Pour half of the batter on top of the crust
- Return container to processor, add the gelatin mixture to the remaining batter and process just until combined – do not over mix – this batter will be a light orange color
- Pour this batter on top of the first layer (in a circular motion) to create a swirl pattern
- Bake for about 1 hour or until you notice that the edges of the cake have risen slightly and are golden brown
- Remove pan from oven and let sit until it is room temperature (about 1½ - 2 hours)
- Place in refrigerator while still in spring form pan for several hours or overnight

Topping

4 ounces cream cheese

⅓ cup powdered sugar

1 teaspoon vanilla extract

½ teaspoon orange extract

2 drops of yellow food coloring

1 drop of red food coloring

1 cup heavy whipping cream

- Put cream cheese, powdered sugar, vanilla and orange extracts and the food colorings in a 1 quart mixing bowl. *Note: using the food colorings is optional; however, it will create a beautiful orange color that will enhance the presentation.*
- Using a hand mixer, whip on high until smooth
- Add heavy whipping cream and whip on high until stiff peaks form

To Serve

1 – 11 ounce can of mandarin oranges

- Remove cheesecake from spring form pan and transfer to platter
- Swirl Chantilly Cream evenly on top of cake
- Drain mandarin oranges and lay on paper towels to thoroughly dry
- Arrange orange sections around the outer edges of the cake

The peanut better and jelly sandwich is the old standby in any school lunch box, so it wasn't a surprise when the customers at my son Joseph's restaurant made a request to re-imagine it as a cheesecake. This is my attempt to satisfy their desires. I have made it using strawberry or raspberry jam and even grape jelly. I'm sure you will use your imagination and try most any flavor you like. Have fun with this one.

Peanut Butter & Jelly

Crust

2 cups graham cracker crumbs
½ cup sugar
1 stick butter, melted

- Combine all dry ingredients in a bowl
- Pour melted butter over dry ingredients
- Mix together until all ingredients are combined
- Using your hands, press mixture evenly into the bottom of a 10 inch spring form pan
- Place spring form pan on top of a cookie sheet or pizza pan - this will prevent butter from dripping onto your oven, set aside

Batter

3 – 8 ounces packages cream cheese
2 cups sour cream
1 – 14 ounce can sweetened condensed milk
1 tablespoon vanilla extract
5 large eggs
½ cup peanut butter (smooth or crunchy)
½ cup of your favorite jam or preserves (not jelly)
1-2 drops food coloring (optional)

- Preheat oven to 350 degrees
- Using at least a 10 cup capacity food processor, place all ingredients EXCEPT 1 of the eggs, peanut butter and jam or preserves into the work bowl
- Process on high for about 1-2 minutes or until batter is smooth and lump free
- While still processing mixture, start adding the eggs (4 of the 5) - one at a time
- Please know that to achieve best results, you will need to stop processing, remove top of machine, and using a spatula, scrape down the sides of the work bowl and check for lumps
- Continue to process mixture until it is smooth and free of lumps
- Pour about half of this batter into a separate mixing bowl leaving the other half in the food processor
- Add the jam or preserves (and food coloring if desired) to the mixture remaining in the food processor
- Process until totally smooth and well incorporated
- Pour this mixture on top of the crust
- Return the batter that is in the mixing bowl to the food processor and add the peanut butter and the last egg.
- Process until smooth and well incorporated – this will be a very thick batter and may not pour easily
- Using a circular motion pour this batter on top of the batter that is already in your pan
- Bake for about 1 hour or until you notice that the edges of the cake have risen slightly and are golden brown
- Remove pan from oven and let sit until it is room temperature (about 1½ - 2 hours)
- Place in refrigerator while still in spring form pan for several hours or overnight

Topping

⅓ cup peanut butter
⅓ cup jam or preserves

- Remove cheesecake from spring form pan and transfer to platter
- Put peanut butter in a small microwavable container and heat for 20 – 30 seconds – peanut butter will be very thin and easy to work with
- Immediately pour melted peanut butter over the top of the cake and quickly spread to cover
- Put jam or preserves in a small microwavable container and heat for 20 – 30 seconds - this will also be very thin and smooth
- Using a small spoon, drop small amounts of the melted jam or preserves over the top of the peanut butter

To Serve

- You can serve immediately or after chilled
- I've used strawberry, raspberry and grape jam and all have turned out wonderful

Hayrides, campfires and s'mores go hand in hand. Both kids and adults love the toasted, sticky marshmallow topping of this dessert. The warm, chocolate ganache add to the authenticity of the original campfire treat. Whether you serve it by the fire pit or the fireplace, be prepared for fond childhood memories.

S'more

Served With Chocolate Ganache

Crust

2 cups graham cracker crumbs
½ cup sugar
1 stick butter melted

- Combine all dry ingredients in a bowl
- Pour melted butter over dry ingredients
- Mix together until all ingredients are combined
- Using your hands, press mixture evenly into the bottom of a 10 inch spring form pan
- Place spring form pan on top of a cookie sheet or pizza pan - this will prevent butter from dripping onto your oven
- Set aside

Batter

3 – 8 ounces packages cream cheese
2 cups sour cream
1 – 14 ounce can sweetened condensed milk
1 tablespoon vanilla extract
5 large eggs
1 tablespoon instant coffee powder
⅓ cup unsweetened cocoa powder

- Preheat oven to 350 degrees
- Using at least a 10 cup capacity food processor, place all ingredients EXCEPT eggs, instant coffee and cocoa powder into the work bowl
- Process on high for about 1-2 minutes or until batter is smooth and lump free
- While still processing mixture, start adding the eggs - one at a time
- Please know that to achieve best results, you will need to stop processing, remove top of machine, and using a spatula, scrape down the sides of the work bowl and check for lumps
- Continue to process mixture until it is smooth and free of lumps
- Add the instant coffee and cocoa powder to the batter and process until smooth and well incorporated
- Pour the batter over the crust
- Bake for about 1 hour or until you notice that the edges of the cake have risen slightly and are golden brown
- Remove pan from oven and let sit until it is room temperature (about 1½ - 2 hours)
- Place in refrigerator while still in spring form pan for several hours or overnight

Topping

⅓ cup evaporated milk or heavy cream
1 tablespoon butter
1 cup semi-sweet chocolate chips

- Remove cheesecake from spring form pan and transfer to platter
- Using a small sauce pan heat milk or cream and butter over medium heat until hot but not boiling
- Remove from heat and add chocolate chips – whisk until chocolate has melted and is smooth
- Immediately pour chocolate ganache over cheesecake and spread evenly

To Serve

1 bag miniature marshmallows

- Slice and plate individual pieces then generously top each piece with miniature marshmallows
- Using a kitchen torch toast the marshmallows until slightly browned
- Alternatively you can place pieces under the broiler of your oven – watch carefully – this only takes a few seconds
- Serve immediately

The inspiration to make this cheesecake was of course, a traditional caramel apple. The fall season was approaching and I could feel and smell the weather change. Kids were going back to school, Halloween was right around the corner, and all you could see in the local markets were beautiful apples of all colors with bags of caramels surrounding them. It was as if they were screaming, "Please take me home and make a treat!" I always listen to food when it speaks to me. As I gazed over the shiny apples and the buttery caramels, the idea of turning them into a cheesecake was a natural choice for me. This cheesecake is a gooey autumn treat for adults and children.

Caramel Apple — Served With Burnt Caramel Sauce

Crust

2 cups graham cracker crumbs
½ cup sugar
1 stick butter melted

- Combine all dry ingredients in a bowl
- Pour melted butter over dry ingredients
- Mix together until all ingredients are combined
- Using your hands, press mixture evenly into the bottom of a 10 inch spring form pan
- Place spring form pan on top of a cookie sheet or pizza pan - this will prevent butter from dripping onto your oven
- Set aside

Batter

3 – 8 ounces packages cream cheese
2 cups sour cream
1 – 14 ounce can sweetened condensed milk
1 tablespoon vanilla extract
4 large eggs
1-21 ounce can apple pie filling

- Preheat oven to 350 degrees
- Using at least a 10 cup capacity food processor, place all ingredients EXCEPT eggs and apple pie filling into the work bowl
- Process on high for about 1-2 minutes or until batter is smooth and lump free
- While still processing mixture, start adding the eggs - one at a time
- Please know that to achieve best results, you will need to stop processing, remove top of machine, and using a spatula, scrape down the sides of the work bowl and check for lumps
- Continue to process mixture until it is smooth and free of lumps
- Pour about ¾ of the batter on top of crust
- With a spoon, gently drop apple pie filling evenly over the batter – do not spread!
- Pour the remaining batter over the top of the filling – some of the filling may be showing and that is ok
- Bake for about 1 hour or until you notice that the edges of the cake have risen slightly and are golden brown
- Remove pan from oven and let sit until it is room temperature (about 1½ - 2 hours)
- Place in refrigerator while still in spring form pan for several hours or overnight

Topping

- Follow directions for burnt camel sauce on next page.

To Serve

Burn Caramel Sauce (recipe on next page)
½ cup toasted, chopped pecans

- Carefully remove cheesecake from spring form pan and transfer to platter
- Pour burnt caramel sauce while still warm over cold cheesecake and sprinkle with pecans. *Note: if sauce is too firm to pour, microwave for a few seconds*
- OPTION: By omitting the apple pie filling and sprinkling additional sea salt over the top of the caramel and pecan topping, you will have a Salted Caramel Pecan Cheesecake

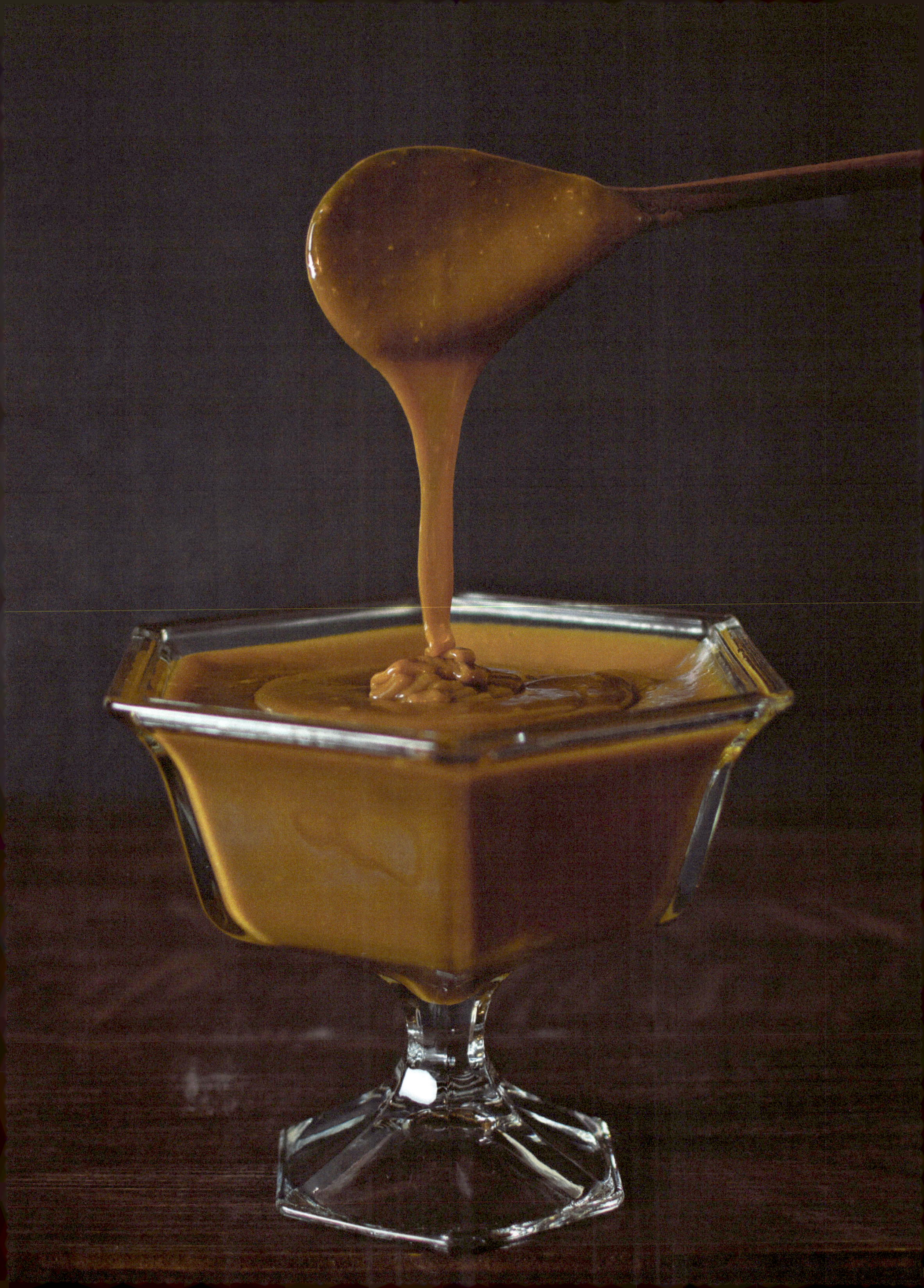

Recipe For Burnt Caramel Sauce

Ingredients

1 cup sugar
2 tablespoons butter
1 teaspoon vanilla extract
1 cup heavy cream
⅛ teaspoon sea salt

Over medium heat, in a non-stick skillet, slowly heat sugar

Using a wooden spoon, stir gently allowing the sugar to melt evenly and become an amber hued liquid – this should take 5 – 10 minutes

Remove from heat, add butter, vanilla extract and cream stirring constantly until mixture is thick and smooth

Add sea salt and stir gently. You can make this ahead of time – it stores nicely in a glass jar

Special Thanks

To my wonderful husband for all of his support and patience and to my family and friends for their ideas and enthusiasm. I think that sometimes they were more excited about this project than I was. It is truly a blessing to have people in your life that love and care about you.

I do want to give a special thanks to:

Carolyn Fielding, a dear friend for decades - we have been through the thick and the thin of life together.

Janet Goldberg, my sister - who was a cheerleader throughout this process and encouraged me daily.

Joan Stockton, another dear friend – whose elegant taste helped create each special display.

Jill Mansfield, my photographer - who made this project a fun experience. We worked together beautifully.

Melissa Lindley – who coordinated a thousand emails and put the final product it all together.

Buffy Davis – who helped with the finishing touches.

Renee Cavanaugh, my daughter – who helped me stay focused when things got overwhelming.

And to the patrons and employees of my son's restaurant "London's" for their continued support and enjoyment of my recipes.

Photographer Jill Mansfield

Jill Mansfield created Grass Roots Photography eight years ago. Her Kentucky roots not only inspired her business name but has also inspired Jill as an artist.

Jill specializes in Senior Photography but has always wanted to pursue Food Photography. Her shooting for Susan's cookbook has been a dream come true.

Jill also enjoys teaching photography to kids and aspiring artists when she is not shooting. Jill loves spending time with her husband, Dan and her daughter, Chloe.

CPSIA information can be obtained
at www.ICGtesting.com
Printed in the USA
BVHW021112131218
535225BV00032B/166/P